THE CONCEPT OF ACTION

When people do things with words, how do we know what they are doing? Many scholars have assumed a category of things called actions: 'requests', 'proposals', 'complaints', 'excuses'. The idea is both convenient and intuitive, but, as this book argues, it is a spurious concept of action. In interaction, a person's primary task is to decide how to respond, not to label what someone just did. The labelling of actions is a meta-level process, appropriate only when we wish to draw attention to others' behaviours in order to quiz, sanction, praise, blame, or otherwise hold them to account. This book develops a new account of action grounded in certain fundamental ideas about the nature of human sociality: that social conduct is naturally interpreted as purposeful; that human behaviour is shaped under a tyranny of social accountability; and that language is our central resource for social action and reaction.

N. J. Enfield is Professor of Linguistics at the University of Sydney, and director of the Sydney Social Sciences and Humanities Advanced Research Centre (SSSHARC). His work on language and human sociality is based on regular fieldwork in mainland Southeast Asia, especially Laos. Among his more recent books are *Relationship Thinking: Agency, Enchrony, and Human Sociality* (2013), *Natural Causes of Language* (2014), *The Utility of Meaning* (2015), and *The Cambridge Handbook of Linguistic Anthropology* (Cambridge, 2014, co-edited with Paul Kockelman and Jack Sidnell).

Jack Sidnell is Professor in the Department of Anthropology at the University of Toronto. His research focuses on the structures of talk and interaction. In addition to research in the Caribbean and Vietnam, he has examined talk in court and among young children. He is the author of *Conversation Analysis: An Introduction* (2010), the editor of *Conversation Analysis: Comparative Perspectives* (Cambridge, 2009) and co-editor of *Conversational Repair and Human Understanding* (Cambridge, 2013), *The Handbook of Conversation Analysis* (2012), and *The Cambridge Handbook of Linguistic Anthropology* (Cambridge, 2014).

NEW DEPARTURES IN ANTHROPOLOGY

New Departures in Anthropology is a book series that focuses on emerging themes in social and cultural anthropology. With original perspectives and syntheses, authors introduce new areas of inquiry in anthropology, explore developments that cross disciplinary boundaries, and weigh in on current debates. Every book illustrates theoretical issues with ethnographic material drawn from current research or classic studies, as well as from literature, memoirs, and other genres of reportage. The aim of the series is to produce books that are accessible enough to be used by college students and instructors, but will also stimulate, provoke, and inform anthropologists at all stages of their careers. Written clearly and concisely, books in the series are designed equally for advanced students and a broader range of readers, inside and outside academic anthropology, who want to be brought up-to-date on the most exciting developments in the discipline.

Series editorial board

The Concept of Action

N. J. ENFIELD
University of Sydney

JACK SIDNELL
University of Toronto

CAMBRIDGE
UNIVERSITY PRESS

University Printing House, Cambridge CB2 8BS, United Kingdom

One Liberty Plaza, 20th Floor, New York, NY 10006, USA

477 Williamstown Road, Port Melbourne, VIC 3207, Australia

4843/24, 2nd Floor, Ansari Road, Daryaganj, Delhi – 110002, India

79 Anson Road, #06–04/06, Singapore 079906

Cambridge University Press is part of the University of Cambridge.

It furthers the University's mission by disseminating knowledge in the pursuit of education, learning, and research at the highest international levels of excellence.

www.cambridge.org
Information on this title: www.cambridge.org/9780521895286
DOI: 10.1017/9781139025928

© N. J. Enfield and Jack Sidnell 2017

First published 2017

Printed in the United Kingdom by Clays, St Ives plc

A catalogue record for this publication is available from the British Library.

Library of Congress Cataloging-in-Publication Data
NAMES: Enfield, N. J., 1966– author. | Sidnell, Jack, author.
TITLE: The concept of action / N.J. Enfield, University of Sydney,
Jack Sidnell, University of Toronto.
DESCRIPTION: Cambridge, United Kingdom ; New York, NY : Cambridge
University Press, 2017. | Series: New departures in anthropology | Includes
bibliographical references and index.
IDENTIFIERS: LCCN 2017014909 | ISBN 9780521895286 (alk. paper)
SUBJECTS: LCSH: Social interaction. | Anthropological linguistics. | Sociolinguistics.
CLASSIFICATION: LCC HM1111 .E535 2017 | DDC 302–dc23
LC record available at https://lccn.loc.gov/2017014909

ISBN 978-0-521-89528-6 Hardback
ISBN 978-0-521-71965-0 Paperback

Contents

Figures and Table

Figures

Table

Preface

If we are to understand human social action, we need to see that language is at the centre of it. By 'language' we mean the directly observable collaborative practices of using words, grammar, and associated semiotic resources, in human interaction. This book is about how people use language to act in the social world, what properties language and human sociality have that make this possible, and how the linguistic nature of action helps us understand the ontology of human agency.

Let us declare some core claims at the outset.

First, we recognize that people have goals, and their behaviour is designed as means towards attaining those goals. The business of knowing what to do in interaction is dependent on working out what other people are doing; and working out what other people are doing is intimately bound up with the task of figuring out their objectives, or at least attributing rational objectives *to* them.[1]

Second, accountability is a definitive element of social action. We can only know what a person has done when we know what a person can be rightly held to account by others for having done.

Third, there is no social accountability – in the core sense of that term – without language. Praising or blaming someone for what they have done is only possible through a description or formulation of 'what they have done'. Such a description is always a *construal*, highlighting some aspects of their behaviour, and bracketing out others. And we emphasize that 'what someone has done' is often something they have

---

[1] This does not mean that people of different cultures cannot have different metacognitive ideologies about intention ascription; clearly, they can (Duranti 2015).

done using language (Austin 1962). So it is not just a fun fact that language is the communication system that can be used to communicate about itself. We constantly use language to talk about or otherwise point to language, from clarifications (*Huh?*) to challenges (*Are you serious?!*) to gossip ('*He-said-she-said*'). When language's definitive properties of displacement (Hockett 1960) and shared intentionality (Tomasello et al. 2005) combine to focus reflexively on language itself, social accountability becomes possible.

In the enchronic flow of language use in interaction, every sign can be read as a response to, and thus a sort of appraisal of, what came before it. This creates in people a constant need to anticipate such responses and to adjust to them pre-emptively in social interaction. In this way, social action is shaped publicly by move and response within the context of a tyranny of accountability.

We shall be considering not just action but actions, distinct acts as moves in social interaction. Social actions are not achieved by one person alone. A social action is consummated by two people together. It is a relation between two people. To have acted socially, a person must succeed in getting another person to come to an appropriate understanding of what they wanted to do, and in turn, in getting that other person to respond in an appropriate way. For an action to be consummated, at least three things must happen: (1) Person A must have made it possible for Person B to ascribe an action to A's behaviour, (2) Person B must have responded in a way that showed evidence of an ascription at some level, and (3) B's responsive move must have been subsequently 'allowed through' (i.e., not contested) and thus implicitly ratified.

In this book we focus on actions as carried out by individual moves, and carried off by dyads enacting social relationships, but just as important are the distributed contextual ecologies in which action emerges (Goodwin 2000), as well as the higher-level motivations and goals, the overarching 'projects' as they are sometimes called (Levinson 2012), which subsume move-level actions as means to ends. We often need to know people's global goals before we can properly interpret their local actions, as, for instance, if somebody asks *Where does she live now?* – our response may be significantly different depending on whether we think the speaker is asking this because they want a general update on the person's life, or because they want their address in order to send them a postcard. We usually have robust intuitions as to what others are trying to do. And we are neither reticent nor unskilled in exercising those intuitions.

While we speak of actions in the plural, we want to be very clear that actions are not selected from an inventory or vocabulary. Actions are not like words. They are more like sentences. Actions are built and achieved in the moment. They are often unique. Interpreting another's behaviour as an action essentially means figuring out how to respond to it appropriately, and this does not mean identifying 'which action it is' from a list. Actions are not necessarily labelled or 'identified' at any level whatsoever. We argue that they are constituted emergently by relations between moves in the enchronic progression of social interaction. That said, given the constantly recurring need to pursue certain social goals over and over again in social life (e.g., getting people to pass you things, or to repeat what they just said), many actions emerge in similar ways, time after time. This means that it is sometimes methodologically convenient to speak of actions of certain kinds – 'request', 'promise', 'compliment', 'complaint' – suggesting a list or inventory of actions. But while such a usage is often methodologically convenient, this does not mean it is theoretically justified to think of action as a matter of selecting from a pre-existing list.

A final preliminary point is that the question of social action must be viewed as an anthropological question; one that investigates issues of diversity and universality within our species. We shall see that while there is diversity in the domain of social action, it is not unconstrained. There are constraints that account for why we have the commonalities we have across cultures and language communities. These come from basic semiotic properties of language, basic structural properties of conversation, and basic features of human sociality. We will be exploring these properties throughout the book.

The title of this book echoes that of Gilbert Ryle's 1949 classic, *The Concept of Mind*, in which he delivers a devastating critique of Cartesian dualism and the presuppositions about mental life upon which it is based. Central to his argument is the proposal that the 'official doctrine' about the mind rests on a host of category errors that have the effect of sustaining the illusion of mental processes, distinct from intelligent acts, that are animated by a ghost in the machine. The implication of Ryle's argument is that philosophical ideas about the mind and mental states as the shadowy causes of conduct involve an unwarranted prioritizing of the theoretical over the practical: 'knowing how' is always treated as derivative of a more fundamental 'knowing that'. But of course the master chef does not work from recipes, and the speaker of a language does not require a dictionary or compendium (mental or otherwise) of grammatical rules (see Tanney 2009). Practical skills, such as cooking a meal or speaking a language, draw upon savoir-faire. Ryle proposed that an 'intellectualist legend' imputes a base of propositional knowledge to all intelligent behaviour and in so doing leads to problems of mind–body dualism and infinite regress. Moreover, within such a conceptual framework, the analyst is led to ask otherwise absurd questions such as what inner events or happenings 'mental predicates' (e.g., 'think', 'believe', 'understand') might refer to.

In many ways, our arguments about action run exactly parallel to Ryle's arguments about mind. We suggest that philosophers and others have created a spurious (though both convenient and intuitive) category of things called actions that are distinct from, and causally related to, the specific practices of conduct and modes of inference through which these 'actions' are realized in interaction. Guided mostly by the metalinguistic vocabulary of ordinary language, scholars in various traditions have argued or assumed that it should be possible to arrive at a list or inventory of possible action types, and that if a person wants to accomplish one or other of them, they merely need to provide adequate cues as to which one of these possible actions they mean to be doing. In our view this is a wrongheaded notion of action. As we will see in the following chapters, this supposes an ontology of actions akin to the phonemes that constitute the phonological inventory of a language.

On our view, by contrast, an action need not be nameable at all. When an action is named, this is always a construal or, in the sense of Anscombe (1957, 1979), a description of behaviour that is realized in and through (folk or academic) practices of linguistic formulation. But interaction does not require descriptive construal of others' moves, and participants are perfectly able to carry on without, for the most part, recourse to action formulations. Rather than deciding *what* a bit of behaviour was, what people must decide is how to respond to it, drawing on the affordances of others' behaviour, and the available inferences as to what those others are doing. Such doings are seldom tokens of types.

At base, the idea of action seems simple. Action is controlled behaviour that is carried out as means to ends and that can be interpreted as having reasons: for example, picking up a glass to drink from it because you're thirsty, turning a door handle to open it because you want to go outside, lighting a cigarette to smoke it, waving to someone across the room, asking someone the time (Anscombe 1957; Davidson 1963, 1978). As the sociologist Alfred Schutz defined it, action is 'spontaneous activity oriented toward the future' (Schutz 1967:57). Schutz then defined *rational* action as 'action with known intermediate goals' (Schutz 1967:61). This sounds simple, but how do we know whether a given action is controlled and ends-directed? How do we know its reasons?

An important resource we have here is to be found in the responses that an action elicits, or can be expected to elicit. This is why the interpreter or addressee has a privileged role in the notion of communicative action being developed in this book. It is why conversation analysts advise us to look at interpreters' responses to moves in interaction if we want evidence for what those moves mean (Schegloff and Sacks 1973:299; Sacks, Schegloff, and Jefferson 1974:728–9). It is why we are advised to look at a move and ask 'Why that now?': not just because we can, but because it is a question that participants in interaction are asking themselves.

All action is potentially communicative and, where the situation allows for observation by others, is designed with an eye to how it will be understood by others (see Sacks 1995 on observability; see also Kidwell and Zimmerman 2006; Kidwell 2011). Thus, a child who fears she may be held accountable for another child's distress may hammer a pretend block with extra, visible concentration to obscure the fact that just minutes before she used the same toy to hit the crying child on the head (Kidwell 2011). A person standing at a corner, waiting to cross the street may organize her body to convey this intention to whoever may be looking. Another person waiting at the same corner for a friend will organize her body in a quite different way, in part to defeat the inference that she means to cross the street.

At the same time, all communication is action. No form of communication involves the mere passing of information. When a voice comes over the loudspeaker in an airport informing passengers that the plane is now ready to board, the airline is alerting those persons who are waiting, perhaps allaying fears that the flight might be further delayed or encouraging them to ready themselves for boarding. Expressions such as *I'm just telling you how it sounds* and *I'm just saying* are scattered across recordings of English conversation (and presumably roughly similar expressions are found in the conversational recordings of other languages), but it is in fact impossible for an utterance to merely inform without at the same time also accomplishing other actions beyond 'just saying'.

A radical rethinking of the relationship between language and action is needed. While language does make possible a direct formulation of the actions that speakers mean to perform ('She requested some leaf' and so on), the truth is that linguistic formulation is, ultimately, incidental to whatever action might actually be performed. Language is one means by which speakers can provide evidence to others of what it is they mean to do. Importantly, the evidence it provides is never definitive. Even on the telephone, where the medium of communication seems to be reduced to the linguistic channel, the utterance is accompanied by non-linguistic forms of information which provide evidence to a recipient/hearer about what it is a speaker is doing with each move. And even where the linguistic formulation seems to point in a direct way to the action being attempted, things frequently (indeed, we would suggest, inevitably) turn out to be more complicated. Someone who says *I'll bet it's a dream* is likely not offering to make a wager, just as someone who says *Do you want me to come and get her?* is probably not just asking a question about what the recipient wants.

There are three things we have to keep in mind when we think about action. For any piece of behaviour that might constitute an action, here are the three things that matter: (1) the composition of the behaviour, (2) the context of the behaviour, and (3) the position of the behaviour in a communicative sequence. Composition, context, and position. We introduce what we mean by these three things in Chapter 1, and the ideas are explicated further through the book.

There is a thread that runs through these three things, drawing them together, at all points. That thread is social accountability. We cannot emphasize enough the importance of social accountability to what we are trying to say in this book. As sociologists including Garfinkel, Goffman, and Sacks have shown, people's knowledge that they are potentially accountable for any move they make is what leads them to 'act normal' – i.e. to act in such a way as to avoid appearing abnormal and thereby avoid generating inferences about what that departure from the normal might mean. Accountability is what defines the normatively appropriate selection of semiotic resources in composing behaviour for action, the normatively appropriate positioning of that behaviour in sequences of interaction, and our subprehension (or 'anticipation', conscious or not) of how our behaviour will be responded to, and, potentially, described and evaluated.

There is a tyranny of accountability in human social life. It provides us with the coordinates for seeing meaning in others' behaviour, for planning our own behaviour in anticipation of how others will see it, and thus for the design and interpretation of every next move in the progression of social life.

Acknowledgements

We gratefully acknowledge the following funding support: European Research Council grant 240853, University of Sydney Bridging Grants (2015 and 2016), and a University of Sydney Quality Publication Incentive Grant (2016).

Some sections of this book are based on materials drawn from the following works: N. J. Enfield (2013), *Relationship Thinking*, Oxford University Press; N. J. Enfield (2014b), 'Human agency and the infrastructure for requests', in Paul Drew and Elizabeth Couper-Kuhlen, eds., *Requesting in Social Interaction*, pp. 35–50, John Benjamins; J. Sidnell and N. J. Enfield (2014), 'The ontology of action, in interaction', in N. J. Enfield, P. Kockelman, and J. Sidnell, eds., *The Cambridge Handbook of Linguistic Anthropology*, pp. 423–46, Cambridge University Press; J. Sidnell and N. J. Enfield (2012), 'Language diversity and social action: A third locus of linguistic relativity', *Current Anthropology* 53(3):302–33.

We acknowledge with gratitude our enormous debt to the many colleagues, students, and friends who have taught us so much about the concept of action.

Abbreviations

1SG	first person singular pronoun
1SG.BARE	first person singular pronoun, bare
1SG.POL	first person singular pronoun, polite
2SG.POL	second person singular pronoun, polite
2PL.BARE	second person plural pronoun, bare
3SG	third person singular pronoun
3SG.BARE	third person singular pronoun, bare
3SG.POL	third person singular pronoun, polite
3PL.BARE	third person plural pronoun, bare
ADE	adessive case
CLF	classifier
CLI	clitic
COP	copula
CT.FAMIL	class term, familiar
DEM.ACROSS	demonstrative, across
DEM.DIST	demonstrative, distal
DEM.EXT	demonstrative, external
DEM.NONPROX	demonstrative, non-proximal
DEM.PROX	demonstrative, proximal
DEM.UP	demonstrative, uphill/upstream
eB	elder brother
ESS	essive case
FAC.INFORM	factive marker, informing
FAC.PRF	factive marker, perfect
HES	hesitation marker

List of Abbreviations

ILL	illative case
IMP.GO	imperative, go and do it
IMP.SOFT	imperative, soft
IMP.UNIMP	imperative, action unimpeded
INTJ	interjection
IRR	irrealis
LOC	locative
M.BARE	male title, bare
MeZ	mother's older sister
NEG	negation
PRED	predicative marker
PAR	partitive case
PRT	particle
PRF	perfect
QPLR	polar question marker
QPLR.PRESM	polar question marker, truth presumed
QPLR.INFER	polar question marker, proposition inferred
TLNK	topic linker
TPC	topic
TPC.DIST	topic, distal

Transcription Conventions

[Separate left square brackets, one above the other on two successive lines with utterances by different speakers, indicate a point of overlap onset, whether at the start of an utterance or later.

]   Separate right square brackets, one above the other on two successive lines with utterances by different speakers, indicate a point at which two overlapping utterances both end or where one ends while the other continues, or simultaneous moments in overlaps which continue.

=   Equal signs ordinarily come in pairs, one at the end of a line, and another at the start of the next line or one shortly thereafter. They are used to indicate two things:

    (1) If the two lines connected by the equal signs are by the same speaker, then there was a single, continuous utterance with no break or pause, which was broken up in order to accommodate the placement of overlapping talk.

    (2) If the lines connected by two equal signs are by different speakers, then the second followed the first with no discernible silence between them, or was 'latched' to it.

(1.0)   Numbers in parentheses indicate silence, represented in tenths of a second; what is given here in the left margin

	indicates 1.0 seconds of silence. Silences may be marked either within an utterance or between utterances.
(.)	A dot in parentheses indicates a 'micropause', hearable, but not readily measurable without instrumentation; ordinarily less than 0.2 of a second.
. ? ,	Punctuation marks are not used grammatically, but to indicate intonation. The period indicates a falling, or final, intonation contour, not necessarily the end of a sentence. Similarly, a question mark indicates rising intonation, not necessarily a question, and a comma indicates 'continuing' intonation, not necessarily a clause boundary.
:	Colons are used to indicate the prolongation or stretching of the sound just preceding them. The more colons, the longer the stretching.
-	A hyphen after a word or part of a word indicates a cut-off or self-interruption, often done with a glottal or dental stop.
word	Underlining is used to indicate some form of stress or emphasis, by either increased loudness or higher pitch. The more underlining, the greater the emphasis.
WOrd	Especially loud talk may be indicated by upper case; again, the louder, the more letters in upper case. In extreme cases, upper case may be underlined.
°	The degree sign indicates that the talk following it is markedly quiet or soft.
°word°	When there are two degree signs, the talk between them is markedly softer than the talk around them.
_:	Combinations of underlining and colons are used to indicate intonation contours: If the letter(s) preceding a colon is (are) underlined, then there is an 'inflected' falling intonation contour on the vowel (you can hear the pitch turn downward).

:	If a colon is itself underlined, then there is an inflected rising intonation contour.
↓↑	The up and down arrows mark sharper rises or falls in pitch than would be indicated by combinations of colons and underlining, or they may mark a whole shift, or resetting, of the pitch register at which the talk is being produced.
> <	The combination of 'more than' and 'less than' symbols indicates that the talk between them is compressed or rushed.
< >	Used in the reverse order, they can indicate that a stretch of talk is markedly slowed or drawn out. The 'less than' symbol by itself indicates that the immediately following talk is 'jump-started', i.e. sounds like it starts with a rush.
hh	Hearable aspiration is shown where it occurs in the talk by the letter *h* – the more *h*'s, the more aspiration. The aspiration may represent breathing, laughter, etc. If it occurs inside the boundaries of a word, it may be enclosed in parentheses in order to set it apart from the sounds of the word.
.hh	If the aspiration is an inhalation, it is shown with a dot before it (usually a raised dot) or a raised degree symbol.
( )	Empty parentheses indicate that something is being said, but no hearing (or, in some cases, speaker identification) can be achieved.

Part I

Preliminaries to Action

ONE

Basics of Action

Words are part of action and they are equivalents to actions.

(Malinowski 1935)

The central problem of linguistic pragmatics and the anthropology of language is to understand the relation between speaking and doing, between language and action. Since Austin (1962) it has been widely appreciated that in speaking, persons are inevitably understood to be doing things, yet, somewhat surprisingly, a comprehensive account of just how action is accomplished through the use of language (and other forms of conduct) in interaction has been slow to develop. In this chapter we begin our sketch of an approach to this problem, by pointing to some of the materials that are relevant to such an account, some of the questions that must be addressed, and some of the central conceptual problems that require consideration.

If we are going to understand what human social action is, we must first acknowledge (1) that action is semiotic, i.e., that its formal composition is crucial to its function, because that formal composition is what leads to its ascription by others; (2) that action is strongly contextualized, i.e., that the shared cultural and personal background of interactants can determine, guide, and constrain the formation and ascription of an action; and (3) that action is enchronic, i.e., that it is a product of the norm-guided sequential framework of move and counter-move that characterizes human interaction. In other words, if we are going to understand action, composition matters, context matters, and position matters. We begin with an example that illustrates these three indispensable features of action in interaction.

Consider the following exchange from a small community of people in the Kri-speaking village of Mrkaa in Laos (300 km due east of Vientiane, just inside the Laos-Vietnam border). This recording is a representative sample of the sort of everyday human social reality that we want to explore in this book. Figure 1.1 is from a scene recorded on video on a humid morning in August 2006.

The participants are sitting on the front verandah of the house of the woman named Phừà, the older woman who is sitting at the rightmost of frame. Here are the people in the frame, going from left to right of the image:

Figure 1.1 Screenshot from video recording of Kri speakers in Mrkaa Village, Laos, 8 August 2006 (060808d-0607).

- Sùàj = older woman in foreground, leftmost in image, with headscarf
- Nùàntaa = teenage girl in doorway with her hand raised to her mouth
- Mnee = young girl with short hair, hunched in doorway
- Phiiw = middle-aged woman with black shirt near centre of image (Nùàntaa's mother's older sister)
- Thìn = young mother in background
- Phừà = older woman at right of image with headscarf (Nùàntaa's mother's mother)

The people in Figure 1.1 are speakers of Kri, a Vietic language which is spoken by a total of about 300 upland shifting agriculturalists in the forested vicinity of Mrkaa, a village in Nakai District, Khammouane Province, Laos (Enfield and Diffloth 2009). The time of recording is around 9 o'clock in the morning. The women in Figure 1.1 are just chatting. Some are sitting and doing nothing, others are preparing bamboo strips for basketry.

As the transcription in (1) below shows, at this point in the conversation the two older women, Sùàj and Phừà, are talking about people in the village who have recently acquired video CD players. They are voicing their opinions as to whose CD player is better, and whether they prefer black and white or colour. Our focus of interest for the purposes of our discussion of action is, however, not this trajectory of the conversation but the one that is started in line 13 by the teenage girl Nùàntaa (NT), who sets out to procure some 'leaf', that is, a 'leaf' of corncob husk, for rolling a cigarette. A few moments before this sequence began, Nùàntaa had asked for something to smoke, and was handed some tobacco by Sùàj.

(1) 060808d-06.23-06.50

01   (0.4)

02 Phừà: qaa   tàà   nờờ lêêq sd- sii
           CT.FAMIL DEM.DIST PRT take C-   colour
           It was them who got a C- colour (CD set).

5

03   (1.0)

04 Phừà: sdii   sii
              CD   colour
              A colour CD set.

05   (1.0)

06 Phừà: teeq   kooq   prak   hanq   teeq   dêêh   lêêq
              1SG   have   money 3SG   1SG   NEG   take
              (If) I had money I (would) not take

07   qaa   sdii   (.)   khaaw   dam   naaq
         HES   CD   white   black   DEM.EXT
         um a black and white CD set.

08   (2.7)

09 Sùàj: khaaw   dam   ci   qalêêngq
              white   black   PRED   look
              (With) a black and white (CD set, one can) see

10   môôc   lùùngq   haar   lùùngq=
         one   story   two   story
         one or two stories (only).

11 Phừà: =hak   longq   haj   paj-
              but   CLF   nice   COP
              But the ones that are nice are-

12 Phừà: longq   [tak]   paj   haj
              CLF   correct COP   nice
              The ones that are 'correct' are nice.

13 NT: [naaj]
              MEZ
              Aunty

14   ((0.7; Mnee turns gaze to Phiiw;
         Phiiw does not gaze to Nùàntaa))

15 NT: piin sulaaq laa
          give leaf   PRT
          Please pass some leaf.

16   ((1.0; Mnee keeps gaze on Phiiw;
          Phiiw does not gaze to Nùàntaa))

17 NT: naaj= (('insistent' prosody))
          MEZ
          Aunty!

18 Sùàj: =pii qaa
           like HES
           Like um-

19   (0.5)
          ((Phiiw and Phừà both turn their gaze to Nùàntaa))

20 NT: piin sulaaq
          give leaf
          Pass some leaf.

21 Phừà: sulaaq quu kuloong lêêh,
           leaf   LOC inside   DEM.UP
           The leaf is inside up there,

22   sulaaq, quu khraa seeh
          leaf   LOC store DEM.ACROSS
          the leaf, in the storeroom.

23   (0.7)

24 Phừà: môôc cariit   hanq
           one   backpack 3SG
           (There's) a (whole) backpack.

25   (5.0)
          ((Nùàntaa walks inside in the direction of the storeroom))

7

The course of action that Nùàntaa engages in here, beginning in line 13, is an instance of one of the most fundamental social tasks that people perform: namely, to elicit the cooperation of social associates in pursuing one's goals (see Rossi 2014; and Chapter 3 below). It presupposes that others will cooperate, that they will be willing to help an individual pursue their unilateral goals. This is the most basic manifestation of the human cooperative instinct (Enfield 2014), which is not present in anything like the same way, or to anything like the same degree, in other species (Tomasello 2008). In this case, Nùàntaa is indeed given assistance in reaching her goal – here not by being given the leaf she asks for, but by being told where she can find some.

Now that we have introduced this bit of data drawn from everyday human social life, how, then, are we to approach an analysis of the actions being performed by the people involved?

Social Action Is Semiotic

It is obvious, but still worth saying, that an adequate account of how social actions work must be a semiotic one in that it must work entirely in terms of the available perceptible data. This follows from a no telepathy assumption, as Hutchins and Hazlehurst (1995) term it. If actions can be achieved at all, it must be by means of what is publicly available. More specifically, this requires that we acknowledge the inherently semiotic mode of causation that is involved in social action. When we talk about action here, we are not talking about instrumental actions in which results come about from natural causes. In the example that we are exploring, the girl Nùàntaa launches a course of behaviour that eventually results in her getting hold of the cornhusk that she desired. For a semiotic account of the social actions involved, we need to know how Nùàntaa's behaviour – mostly constituted in this example by acts of vocalization – could have been interpreted by those present, such that it came to have the results it had (namely, that she quickly came into possession of the leaf she was after).

A first, very basic, issue has to do with units. It is commonplace and perhaps commonsensical to assume that a single utterance performs a single action. Whether it is made explicit or not, this is the view of the speech act approach. If something is a promise, for example, it cannot at the same time be, say, a request. However, there are obvious problems with this. For a start, the very notion of an utterance is insufficiently precise. Rather, we have to begin by, at least, distinguishing utterances from the discrete units that constitute them. In the conversation analytic tradition, we can distinguish a turn-at-talk (often roughly equivalent to 'utterance' in other approaches) from the turn-constructional units (or TCUs) of which it is composed (roughly equivalent to 'linguistic item' in other approaches, thus not only words but other meaningful units, some being smaller than a word, some larger; see Sacks et al. 1974; Langacker 1987). A turn may be composed of one, two, or more TCUs, and each TCU may accomplish some action. Consider these lines from our example:

(2) 060808d-06.23-06.50 (extract)

13 NT: [naaj]
                 ᴍ ez
                 Aunty

14   ((0.7; Mnee turns gaze to Phiiw;
              Phiiw does not gaze to Nùàntaa))

15 NT: piin   sulaaq laa
          give   leaf   ᴘ ʀ ᴛ
          Please pass some leaf.

The utterance translated as 'Aunty, please pass some leaf' is composed of two TCUs. In the first TCU (line 13) the speaker uses a kin term, *naaj* '(classificatory) mother's elder sister', to summon one of the co-participants (Schegloff 1968). Notice that this TCU projects more talk to come and with it the speaker obligates herself to produce additional talk directed at the person so addressed (thus a common response to a summons like this might be *What?* or *Hold on*). One cannot summon another person without then addressing them further once their attention has been secured. In the second TCU of this turn, the speaker produces what can, retrospectively, be seen as the reason for the summons: a 'request' that Aunty pass some leaf (this move to be discussed further, below).

This TCU/turn account in which each TCU is understood (by analysts and by the participants) to accomplish a discrete action appears to work reasonably well for the present case, but there are complications. First, there are cases in which a series of TCUs together constitutes an action that is more than the sum of its parts. For instance, a series of TCUs that describe a trouble (e.g., *I've had a long day at work, and there's no beer in the fridge*) may together constitute a complaint (*This is bad, there should be some beer*) or a request (*Could someone get some beer?*; see, e.g., Pomerantz and Heritage 2012). And there are cases in which a single TCU accomplishes multiple actions. Indeed, there are several senses in which this is the case. There is the telescopic sense, whereby a given utterance such as *What is the deal?* constitutes both a question (which makes an answer relevant next) and an accusation (which makes a defence, justification or excuse relevant next), or *That's a nice shirt you're wearing* is both an assessment (saying something simply about my evaluation of the shirt) and a compliment (saying something good about you). It seems obvious in this case that 'assessment' and 'compliment' are not two different things but two ways of construing or focusing on a single thing. Similarly, we might look at a labrador and ask whether it is a 'dog', an 'animal', or a 'pet'. It is of course all of these, and none is more appropriate than the other in any absolute sense.

There is also the possibility that an utterance is ambiguous as to the action it performs, in the sense that an utterance might have two possible action readings but cannot have both at the same time. For example, consider the utterance *Well, I guess I'll see you sometime* said during the closing phase of a telephone call. What is the speaker doing by saying this? It might constitute a guess at some possible future event. Or it could be a complaint about the recipient's failure to make herself available.

And, finally, there is the idea that different actions can be made in parallel, by means of different elements of a single utterance: for example, a given word or phrase, embedded in an utterance meant to accomplish one action, might accomplish another simultaneous action. In one case, a mother has rejected her daughter's request to work in the store, and she explains this rejection by saying *People just don't want* **children** *waiting on them*. With the use of the word 'children' – implying 'you are a child' – she is effectively belittling her daughter in the process of giving an explanation (see discussion of this case in Chapter 4, below).

Much of this follows directly from the semiotic account we are proposing. Specifically, although TCUs may be typically treated as 'single-action-packages', they are in fact outputs/inputs of the turn-taking system (Sacks, Schegloff, and Jefferson 1974) and only contingently linked to the production of action per se. Participants, then, apparently work with a basic heuristic which proposes that one TCU equals one action, but the inference this generates is easily defeated in interaction. The more general point, following directly from the semiotic assumptions of our approach, is that TCUs – and for that matter talk in general along with any other conduct – is nothing more and nothing less than a set of signs that a recipient uses as a basis for inference about what a speaker's goal is in producing the utterance (or, essentially, what the speaker wants to happen as a result of producing the utterance).

Whatever a speaker is understood to be doing is always an inference or guess derived from the perceptible data available. That includes talk, but it includes much else besides. In the case of language, things get complicated (or look complicated to analysts) because the specifically linguistic constituents of conduct appear to allow for a level of explicitness that is unlike anything else. It is as though a speaker can merely announce or describe what they are doing. Moreover, such formulations may be produced at various levels of remove from the conduct they are intended to describe. One can thus distinguish between a reflexive metapragmatic formulation (*I **bet** you he'll run for mayor*) and a reportive metapragmatic formulation (*He **bet** me that he would run for mayor*), and within the latter one can distinguish between distal (as above) and proximate versions (*Oh no I'm serious, I meant to put a wager on it when I said I'll bet you!*), etc. One can already begin to see, however, a major disconnect between action-in-vivo and explicit action formulations using language. Thus, when someone says *I bet you he'll run for mayor*, thereby apparently formulating what they are doing in saying what they are saying, they are almost certainly not betting (in the sense of making a wager) but rather predicting a future state of events.

All of this leads us to the conclusion – originally developed most cogently within conversation analysis (see Schegloff and Sacks 1973 and Schegloff 1993) – that any understanding of what some bit of talk is doing, whether the analyst's or the co-participant's, must take account of both its 'composition' and its 'position'. To take one example, the word *well* can function in different ways depending both on exactly how it is pronounced and on where in an utterance it is placed: thus, using a lengthened *We::ll* at the beginning of a response to a wh-question routinely indicates that something other than a straightforward answer is coming (see Schegloff and Lerner 2009); by contrast, a *well* produced at the end of a stretch of talk on a topic during a telephone call may initiate closing (Schegloff and Sacks 1973).

Social Action Is Always Contextualized

We judge an action according to its background within human life, and this background is not monochrome, but we might picture it as a very complicated filigree pattern, which, to be sure, we can't copy, but which we can recognize from the general impression it makes. The background is the bustle of life. And our concept points to something within this bustle.

(Wittgenstein 1980, §§624–5)

Actions are accomplished against a background of presupposition – what is commonly termed context. There are two basic senses in which this is the case. First, there is context in the sense of an historically constituted linguistic code and set of cultural understandings. Second, there is context in the sense of what someone just said, how the speaker and recipient are related to one another, and what is happening in the immediately available perceptual environment and so on. Context in the first sense is essentially omnirelevant: that /kæt/ means a carnivorous animal often kept as a house pet is a part of the backdrop of any interaction in English. Context in the second sense is more dynamic. Aspects of context can be activated and oriented to by the participants within the unfolding course of interaction (Sidnell 2010b; Enfield 2013), alternatively they can be disattended. Thus, these two aspects of context are fundamentally intertwined, since it is the very cultural understandings in the first sense of context that are activated and made relevant in the second sense of context.

In recent work, attempts have been made to give a systematic account of the way participants assess a given utterance against the backdrop of assumptions in order to understand what action it is meant to accomplish. For instance, Heritage (2012) suggests that a recipient will often draw on assumptions about who knows what (epistemic status) in deciding whether a given utterance is doing an action of 'asking' or one of 'telling'. For instance, a speaker who produces a declaratively formatted utterance describing something about the recipient (e.g., *You're tired*) has conveyed a relatively certain epistemic stance that runs counter to the usual assumptions of epistemic status (i.e., that people know more about how they themselves feel than others do) and thus is likely to be heard as asking rather than telling. Heritage (2012:1) proposes: 'Insofar as asserting or requesting information is a fundamental underlying feature of many classes of social action, consideration of the (relative) epistemic statuses of the speaker and hearer are a fundamental and unavoidable element in the construction of social action.' Roughly speaking, Heritage shows that a recipient's assumptions about what the speaker does or does not know are decisive in determining whether a declaratively formatted utterance is heard to be telling or asking (see also Sidnell 2012b). The idea here, then, is that a given utterance conveys its speaker's epistemic stance and that this is understood against the backdrop of assumptions that constitute epistemic status.

Might such insights be generalized to other domains of action in interaction? For instance, one could suppose that in the case of cooperative action sequences a speaker may convey a deontic stance that will be measured against the relatively stable, enduring assumptions of deontic status. Deontic stance, within this view, names the various ways of coding entitlement and authority in the utterance itself (compare *Get out!* with *Would you mind stepping outside for a minute?*). Deontic status has to do with the relatively perduring assumptions about who is entitled or obligated to do what.

Incongruity between stance and status in this domain has similar inferential consequences as does incongruity in the domain of epistemics. For instance, when a recipient who has just received some surprising bit of news says *Shut up* or *Get out of here*, they are not understood to be issuing a directive but rather conveying surprise or interest (Heritage 2012:570). Inferences are also possible from utterances which adopt a 'D-minus' stance, that is, which are phrased as if the speaker has diminished entitlement to make the action at hand. For example, a parent can convey great seriousness and an unwillingness to negotiate by saying to a child *Will you please stop talking*, as if it were a polite request, or *I'm asking you to finish your dinner*, as if it were a formal statement.

In our example we can see that Nùàntaa's turn, *piin sulaaq laa* 'Please pass some leaf', in line 15, adopts a deontic stance congruent with the assumptions of deontic status: namely, as one of the youngest people on the scene, she is 'below' her addressees in kinship terms, and thus in terms of her entitlements to impose on others with requests such as this one. The summons by means of a kin term in line 13 makes this explicit, marking and thereby activating this aspect of context.

Let us, now, look into our example more closely, to illustrate the necessity of drawing upon the numerous systemic backgrounds against which the participants in this little scene can make sense of it. We start with line 13, in which Nùàntaa launches her course of action with the goal to acquire some leaf for rolling tobacco. The utterance consists of a single word: *naaj*. The only direct translation into English of this word would be 'aunt', but while these words have some overlap in denotational range they are not equivalent. The Kri system of kinship terminology differs from that of English in a range of ways.[1] For one thing, the system makes a great number of distinctions, segmenting the kinship space far more finely than English: compare Figure 1.2 and Figure 1.3.

The action that is done in line 13 is done by means of a single lexical unit, the kin term *naaj* 'mother's older sister'. What action is Nùàntaa performing with this one-word utterance? A basic characterization would be to say it is a summons. It is a first move in opening up the channel for interaction. We do this when we walk into a house and call

---

[1] According to the classification of Morgan's (1997/1871) *Systems of Consanguinity and Affinity of the Human Family*, English kin terminology is a variant of the 'Eskimo' system, whereas Kri kin terminology is of the Sudanese type.

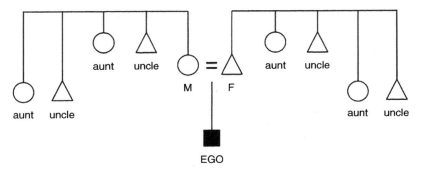

Figure 1.2 English terms for siblings of parents (2 terms, distinguished only by sex of referent); relative height of members of same generation represents relative age (not captured in the meanings of the English terms).

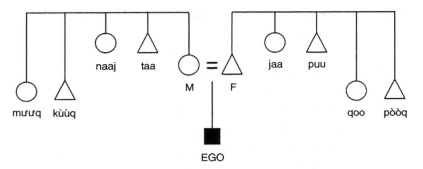

Figure 1.3 Kri terms for siblings of parents (8 terms, distinguished by sex of referent and sex of parent and age of referent relative to parent).

out *Hello?* in order to open up a possible interaction (Clark 1996). Or indeed, and as Schegloff (1968) argues, the ringing of a telephone is a summons as well, and serves a similar function to Nùàntaa's utterance here. But if we compare Nùàntaa's kin-term utterance with the kind of summons that a telephone ring can perform, we see that they have different affordances. One thing that Nùàntaa's specific form of summons does here is to make explicit her kin relation (and thus her social relation) to the addressed party. Clearly other ways of doing the summons were possible (e.g., she might have used the recipient's name) and doing it in this way, rather than another, has a number of collateral effects, as we term them. As we explain in Chapter 4, the selection of a linguistic structure as the means to some end (e.g., summoning a participant by use of a kin term) will inevitably have a range of consequences for which that means was not necessarily selected (e.g., characterizing the relationship between speaker and recipient in terms of kinship rather than in some other available terms).

Chapter 4 compares collateral effects across different linguistic systems, but we can note in passing here that while both Kri *naaj* and English *aunt* characterize the relation between speaker and recipient, the way they do this is different in the two languages. Specifically, while 'aunt' merely conveys that the recipient is the speaker's parent's sister, 'naaj' indicates that the recipient is mother's older sister (and thus a member of the speaker's matrilineage, etc.). So some collateral effects are internal to a specific linguistic system. For instance, had Nùàntaa issued her summons by saying *Hey!* or some such rather than 'naaj', the effects would have been quite different though the action would still be reasonably characterized as summoning (although with some ambiguity as to who she was in fact summoning). Other collateral effects are external to a linguistic system and can only be seen through a comparison of the different semiotic resources they make available for the accomplishment of action.

So there are collateral effects of doing the summons in this way. And the particular effects that arise are not merely incidental. Kri speakers seem especially concerned with kin relations. So with line 13, which is just the opening of Nùàntaa's course of action, and which in itself is purely in the service of that course of action, she has used a single term from a closed class of kin terms to make a summons. The utterance's full action import cannot be understood without the full systemic context of kinship and kin terminology.

Once Nùàntaa has used the term *naaj* to single out Phiiw as her addressee and thereby summon Phiiw's attention, she then produces a next move in her course of action, here what could reasonably be called a request. She does this by naming the action she wants Phiiw to do ('pass') and identifying the thing she wants ('leaf'). This utterance, shown in (3), introduces further aspects of the linguistic system that provides Kri speakers with their resources for social action:

(3) 060808d-06.23-06.50 (extract)

15 NT: piin   sulaaq   laa
        pass   leaf   PRT
        Please pass some leaf.

The turn has several properties worth mentioning in terms of its design or composition:

1. No explicit person reference is used.
2. None of the available alternate constructions are used; e.g., she could have said 'Where can I get some leaf?'
3. The verb choice *piin* 'to pass, present' is chosen instead of the more general word *cɔɔn* 'pass'.
4. The 'polite', 'softening' particle *laa* is used.

The translation here is something like 'Please pass some leaf', and so it seems reasonable to describe it as a request (but see Chapter 4 on the problem of labelling/describing actions, and Chapter 3 on joint action and cooperation specifically). Note, however, that the utterance is not explicitly marked as a request. There is no explicit marking of imperative mood, as, for example, is done in English with the infinitive verb form, nor is the omission of reference to the subject of the verb associated with imperative force in the Kri language. Thus, while it is seemingly clear to the participants that Nùàntaa is asking for something, it is done in a semantically general way. The phrase *piin sulaaq* could, in another context, mean '(He) gave (me) some leaf', or '(I will) give (them) some leaf', among other interpretations. One thing that Nùàntaa does with this format is to leave the interpretation of who is to give leaf to whom entirely dependent on the context. Context is more than strong enough to support the action she is launching here: it is part of the participants' common knowledge that Nùàntaa has, moments before, procured some tobacco, and further, that she has selected Phiiw as the addressee of this utterance.

Another feature of this utterance that cannot be understood without reference to the linguistic system as background context is its value with reference to other ways in which she *could have* produced the utterance. One way, for example, is as a question, for instance *Where is some leaf?* Then there are the specific lexical choices. The thing she is requesting is named by its normal, everyday label *sulaaq*, meaning 'leaf'. She doesn't need to specify 'corncob husk for smoking'. And of relevance to the fact that her action is a request, issued to a superior, is the choice of the verb *piin*. This verb means 'pass' or 'hand over possession of', but it is not the everyday word for 'give' in the mundane sense of handing something over, such as when someone passes someone a knife, a glass of water, or a rag to wipe their hands with. The verb *piin* is more marked, both semantically (by being more specific) and pragmatically (by being used less often and in a narrower range of contexts). And finally, the marker *laa* belongs in a closed class of sentence-final particles, well known in the Southeast Asia region for their importance in marking subtle distinctions in 'sentence type' or speech act function. Notice that the *laa* is omitted when Nùàntaa repeats the request after it has apparently not been heard by Phiiw.

Through this simple example, we can see an important sense then in which social relationships are constituted through action (see Enfield 2013 and references cited therein). Some of it this is obvious, such as, for instance, the ways in which people address each other using kin terms. But many of the ways in which social relations are constituted are less explicit. Following Goffman, we could say that social relations are 'given off' here by the simple fact that the girl is evidently entitled to ask and the recipient is apparently obligated to provide (see Rosaldo 1982; Goodwin 1990). We can note that the addition of *laa* (a polite particle, appropriately used in addressing people who are senior or otherwise deserving of respect) orients to just this relation of entitlement/obligation.

One can easily see the implications of this for linguistics. Specifically, for all of grammar, there is a basic sense in which you cannot understand it unless you understand how it is used in interaction. Elicitation simply does not provide an adequate account of grammatical meaning (elicitation being better suited to the study of grammaticality judgements). Beyond that, though, there are parts of the grammar whose meanings are simply not elicitable.

Now let us consider further the system context as it relates to lines 21–22, the utterance in which Phừà provides the solution to Nùàntaa's problem. Here, Phừà makes good use of the system of spatial demonstratives. Phừà tells Nùàntaa where the leaf is, giving quite specific spatial coordinates relative to where the interlocutors are presently sitting:

(4) 060808d (extract)

| 21 | Phừà: | sulaaq | quu | kuloong | lêêh, |
| | | leaf | LOC | inside | DEM.UP |

The leaf is inside up there,

| 22 | | sulaaq, | quu | khraa | seeh |
| | | leaf | LOC | store | DEM.ACROSS |

the leaf, in the storeroom.

The Kri language has a five-term system of exophoric demonstratives, which is partly built on the Kri speakers' deep-seated orientation to a riverine up-down environment:

(5) a. *nìì*   general ('this', proximal)
    b. *naaq*   external ('that', distal)
    c. *seeh*   across ('yon', far distal)
    d. *côôh*   external, down below
    e. *lêêh*   external, up above

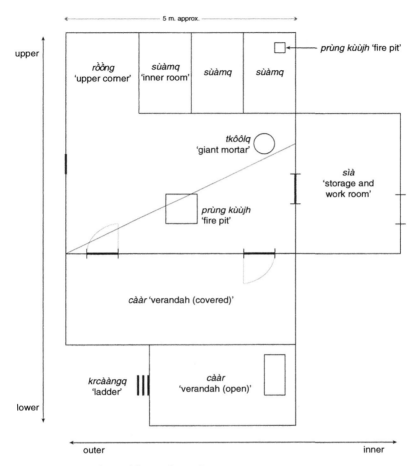

Figure 1.4 Kri traditional house floor plan.

This system for spatial orientation, with its 'up', 'down', and 'across' terms, is used with reference not only to outdoor space but also to local 'table top' space (Levinson and Wilkins 2006). As outlined in Enfield (2013: Chapter 11), the up-down and across axes are mapped onto the Kri traditional house floor plan, as shown in Figure 1.4.

Within this activity of direction-giving, the Kri demonstratives invoke the house structure and its semiotics, relating to the physical environment (see Enfield 2013). For present purposes, we are interested in the action that is being done through this utterance. It is unequivocally an action of 'telling'. More specifically, it is an instruction that helps the recipient to satisfy the goal she has expressed in her turn at line 15 and again at line 20. But notice that this turn could be understood in other ways simultaneously. For instance, Nùàntaa may hear in this a reprimand for asking: 'Don't expect to be given it, go and get it yourself'. Or she may hear this as an expression of permission, essentially equivalent to saying 'You may have some of our household leaf'.

We noted earlier that Nùàntaa's request could have been formulated as a 'Where?' question, but it wasn't. Now see that Phɨ̀à's utterance in line 21 responds to the question precisely as if it had in fact been a 'Where?' question. Phɨ̀à does not respond by giving Nùàntaa some leaf, rather she tells her where some leaf can be found, implying where Nùàntaa can get some herself, and in doing this she addresses Nùàntaa's goal. And note that this further orients to the social relations at hand. Simply telling Nùàntaa where she can get some leaf presumes that she will indeed go and get it herself; were the asker a guest, it is likely that Phiiw would have got up, or got someone else to fetch the leaf.

We can take this analysis one step further to propose that at the heart of this little scene is an issue of propriety. Thus, although the request is done as 'pass' (which focuses on possession transfer), it is treated as 'where?' The response then construes the leaf as already belonging in a certain sense to Nùàntaa; all she has to do is take it.

Position Matters: The Account of Action Must Work in an Enchronic Frame

Any research on human social life must choose one or more of a set of distinct temporal-causal perspectives, each of which will imply different kinds of research question and different kinds of data (Enfield 2014a). For example, there are well-established distinctions such as that between the *phylogenetic* evolution and the *ontogenetic* development of a structure or pattern of behaviour, or that between *diachronic* processes of the linguistic and historical past and the *synchronic* description of linguistic and cultural systems. Then there are perspectives that focus more on the 'experience-near' flow of time, and that lack established terms. The term *microgenetic* is sometimes used for the 'online' processes studied by psychologists by which behaviour emerges moment by moment within the individual. We are interested in something different from this, although it operates at a similar timescale. This is the perspective of *enchrony*, a perspective we argue is a privileged locus for studying social action.

An enchronic account focuses on 'relations between data from neighbouring moments, adjacent units of behaviour in locally coherent communicative sequences' (Enfield 2009:10; see also Enfield 2013:28–35). This means that the account must work in terms of sign-interpretant relations, to put it in neo-Peircean terms (Kockelman 2005). From this perspective, to say that an utterance, as a sign, gives rise to an interpretant is to say that the utterance brings about a swatch of behaviour that follows the utterance (usually, but not necessarily, immediately), *and* where that following swatch of behaviour only makes sense in terms of the utterance it follows. The interpretant is not directly caused by a sign; rather, it orients to the object of that sign, that is, it orients to what the sign stands for. It is important to note that while interpretants are to some extent regimented by norms (see below), there is no one 'correct' interpretant of a sign. Many interpretants are possible.

Consider lines 13 and 14 from our example:

Figure 1.5 (a) Video still coinciding with line 13 in example (6). (b) Video still coinciding with line 14 in example (6).

(6) 060808d (extract)

13   NT: [naaj]
                MEZ
                Aunty

14   ((0.7; Mnee turns gaze to Phiiw;
                  Phiiw does not gaze to Nùàntaa))

In line 13 (see Figure 1.5a), Nùàntaa, sitting inside the doorway, her face visible, says *naaj*, which selects Phiiw, at centre of image in black shirt, her face turned away; within the subsequent second, in line 14 (see Figure 1.5b), Mnee, the child with the white shirt sitting in the doorway, turns her gaze towards Phiiw.

Taking Nùàntaa's utterance *naaj* as a sign, we can see Mnee's subsequent behaviour of turning her gaze as an interpretant of this sign, because the gaze redirection makes sense in so far as it is a reaction to Nùàntaa's utterance, and it 'points' to what Nùàntaa's utterance means. A normative expectation of the sign in line 13, which we have characterized as a summons to Phiiw, is that the addressee of the summons would display her recipiency for what is to come next (Goodwin 1981; Kidwell 1997). This expectation allows us to make sense of Mnee's gaze redirection as an appropriate interpretant of the utterance. We mean it is appropriate in so far as the response is subprehended by the utterance – nobody is surprised when the response happens (see Enfield 2013:23 and 222, fn 28). Note also that sign-interpretant relations are subject to coherent analysis only as long as we specify the framing that we are using. We have just been discussing Mnee's directing of gaze towards Phiiw in Figure 1.5b as an interpretant of Nùàntaa's utterance in Figure 1.5a, but in a subsequent frame, we see that Mnee's directing of gaze is itself a sign. If, for instance, we were to surmise that Mnee was looking to see how Phiiw would react, our surmising would be an interpretant of Mnee's behaviour as itself a sign.

Since each interpretant is then a sign that begets another interpretant in turn, enchronic contexts move ever forward. And this 'progressivity' is evidently the preferred state of affairs (Stivers and Robinson 2006). We see it in the next two lines of our example. While, as we have just seen, one might have expected to see Phiiw make an explicit display of recipiency to Nùàntaa, she in fact did not. This does not mean she is not attending, however, to what Nùàntaa is going to say to her next. Arguably, it is in line with a preference for progressivity that Nùàntaa takes a risk on the chance that Phiiw is not attending (also possibly allowing that non-response was within the bounds for this kind of utterance but not the request; cf. Stivers and Rossano 2010) and instead goes ahead with the explicit request for some leaf. Then, however, in the following moments, as shown again here, Phiiw does not respond at all:

(7) 060808d (extract)

13   NT: [naaj]
               мez
               Aunty

14   ((0.7; Mnee turns gaze to Phiiw;
               Phiiw does not gaze to Nùàntaa))

Figure 1.6 In line 15 (Fig. 1.6a), Nùàntaa produces the explicit request to Phiiw, at centre of image in black shirt, still turned away; in line 16 (Fig. 1.6b), Phiiw does not respond.

15   NT: piin   sulaaq laa
            pass   leaf   PRT
            Please pass some leaf.

16   ((1.0; Mnee keeps gaze on Phiiw;
             Phiiw does not gaze to Nùàntaa))

Line 16 constitutes an 'official absence' of response, a missing interpretant where one was in fact normatively due, or conditionally relevant (Schegloff 1968; Sidnell 2010a). We see evidence of this in that Nùàntaa is demonstrably within her rights to redo the summons that she had first issued at line 13. As shown again here, in (8) below, it is redone in line 17, though this time it can be heard as insistent, done at greater volume, and with a higher and more pronounced falling pitch excursion. Because of this special form, it sounds like it is 'being done for a second time'. As can be seen in Figure 1.7b, this second doing of the summons now does receive the interpretant of 'display of recipiency' that might have been expected in line 14, though it is not only from Phiiw, but Phừà as well (line 19).

(8) 060808d (extract)

15   NT: piin   sulaaq   laa
            pass   leaf   PRT
            Please pass some leaf.

Figure 1.7 In line 17 (Fig. 1.7a), Nùàntaa redoes the summons, this time more 'insistently'; in line 19 (Fig. 1.7b), both Phiiw and Phừà turn their gaze to Nùàntaa, and it is with this configuration in place that Nùàntaa makes the request for the second time (*piin sulaaq* in line 20).

16   ((1.0; Mnee keeps gaze on Phiiw;
                Phiiw does not gaze to Nùàntaa))

17 NT: naaj= (('insistent' prosody))
            ᴍᴇᴢ
            Aunty!

18 Sùàj: =pii qaa
             like   ʜᴇꜱ
            Like um-

19   (0.5)
            ((Phiiw and Phừà both turn their gaze to Nùàntaa))

Note how Phiiw's behaviour of sitting doing nothing becomes meaningful in an enchronic context, quite unlike her behaviour of sitting doing nothing prior to line 13. Nùàntaa's insistent-sounding redoing of the summons in line 17 is an interpretant of this 'sign', i.e., the behaviour of not doing anything at all in line 16.

Now that Nùàntaa has the recipiency of Phiiw and Phừà, she produces the request again, and then, in line 21, Phiiw and Phừà produce two different interpretants to Nùàntaa's sign in line 20. Phiiw's is an energetic interpretant: she feels in her pockets, as if to check whether she has any leaf at hand to give to Nùàntaa. Phừà's is a representational interpretant: she produces a linguistic utterance[2] that states where some leaf is (see Kockelman 2005; Enfield 2013), as shown in (9):

(9) 060808d (extract)

19   (0.5)
           ((Phiiw and Phừà both turn their gaze to Nùàntaa))

20 NT: piin   sulaaq
           pass   leaf
           Pass some leaf.

21 Phừà: sulaaq   quu   kuloong   lêêh,
            leaf   LOC   inside   DEM.UP
            The leaf is inside up there,

22   sulaaq,   quu   khraa   seeh
           leaf   LOC   store   DEM.ACROSS
           the leaf, in the storeroom.

Again, we see the importance of the enchronic frame, and the notion that an utterance can be understood when it is seen as an interpretant of a prior sign. Any understanding of line 21 depends on the fact that it is placed right after the request in line 20. It is dependent on its *position* for what it does (i.e., as an instruction). Otherwise Phừà is just saying where some leaf is.

So we can see that in so far as each interpretant is itself a sign (or better, gives rise to another sign) each turn-at-talk is a kind of join in an architecture of intersubjectivity (see Heritage 1984; Sidnell 2014). So, for example, the talk at line 21 is an interpretant of the request, and it is

---

[2] We note that even though Phừà was not the one who was addressed, she is evidently within her rights to respond. Stivers and Robinson (2006) suggest that a preference for progressivity can license a non-addressed person to respond when an addressed person has clearly experienced trouble in doing so (all things being equal, given the relevant rights and duties), thus allowing the interaction to move forward.

Figure 1.8 In line 21, while Phiiw can be seen putting her hand into her pocket, as if to check whether she has any leaf at hand, Phừà responds verbally with a statement of the location of some leaf. At the beginning of line 21, Phừà is already turning her gaze back to her activity of preparing bamboo strips for basketry work.

in turn (eventually)[3] responded to by Nùàntaa's getting up to follow the instruction to get some leaf herself.

(10) 060808d (extract)

21	Phừà:	sulaaq	quu	kuloong	lêêh,
		leaf	LOC	inside	DEM.UP

The leaf is inside up there,

22		sulaaq,	quu	khraa	seeh
		leaf	LOC	store	DEM.ACROSS

the leaf, in the storeroom.

---

[3] In this respect we can note that response is pursued by the unattached NP, *môôc cariit hanq* 'one backpack' (see Ford, Fox, and Thompson 2002).

23   (0.7)

24 Phừà: môôc   cariit   hanq
            one   backpack   3SG
            (There's) a (whole) backpack.

25   (5.0)
            ((Nùàntaa walks inside in the direction of the storeroom))

With the talk at line 23, Phừà adds a specification of what it is the recipient Nùàntaa should look for. This addition, which by its positioning appears to pursue response, could have been meant simply to help Nùàntaa locate the object (i.e., comparable to the instruction to 'look for a backpack, not loose leaves'). But let us also note that by adding 'whole backpack', Phừà counteracts the underlying 'giving' assumption of the original request – it implies that 'there's plenty' and therefore that there is no need to ask (the leaves represent a common and not an individual property).

We have tracked one line of action here; clearly there are others. We do not want to imply that there's only one trajectory; rather, we see multiple lines of action unfolding simultaneously without that causing a problem for the participants. For example, while Nùàntaa is pursuing leaves to use in the preparation of a smoke, continuing talk is interspersed. At the same time, the smaller child is tracking the action throughout and thereby producing a kind of sub-action of 'observation' manifest in gaze redirection throughout.

Summary

By focusing in this opening chapter on a simple but illustrative example, we have pointed to the idea that actions gain their meaning and function from multiple sources simultaneously. We have explicated this in terms of three injunctions:

1. See that action is semiotic, i.e., it must be made publicly recognizable through some formal means.
2. See that action is culturally contextualized, i.e., actions are generated and interpreted against the shared background of participants in interactions.
3. See that action is enchronic, i.e., actions arise in sequences of move and counter-move, where each action stands as both a response to something, and a thing in need of response.

These points are central to much of what we will say in subsequent chapters. Now before moving to the core of the book in Parts II and III, we broaden our preliminary discussion of the concept of action, turning in Chapter 2 to some previous scholarship on action that supplies points of reference for our argument.

TWO

ॐ

The Study of Action

It is easy to imagine a language consisting only of orders and reports in battle. – Or a language consisting only of questions and expressions for answering Yes and No – and countless other things. – And to imagine a language means to imagine a form of life.

(Wittgenstein 1953, §19)

How could human behavior be described? Surely only by sketching the actions of a variety of humans, as they are all mixed up together. What determines our judgment, our concepts and reactions, is not what <u>one</u> man is doing <u>now</u>, an individual action, but the whole hurly-burly of human actions, the background against which we see an action.

(Wittgenstein 1967, §567)[1]

Language, Action, and Anthropology

Despite Malinowski's programmatic statements, we contend that anthropology has never properly taken account of the fact that language is an instrument of social action (and interaction). In the sub-discipline named linguistic anthropology, the focus has rather been on the relation between language and thought (and the consequences of linguistic diversity for thinking) and, more recently, on the maintenance of social reality and social relations through language and speaking. In the past

---

[1] See also Wittgenstein 1980, Vol. II, §629.

twenty years or so, there has been a marked shift from a focus on language in use (in, e.g., the paradigm of ethnography of speaking) to a focus on people's ideas about language (generally or language in use) under the guise of what are known as language ideologies.

Somewhere in all of this, an anthropological account of language as action got lost, or was never fully established. There has been, to be sure, a great deal of concern with semiotic effectiveness (see, e.g., Silverstein 1976; Fleming and Lempert 2014), but this, we argue, does not deliver an account of action in social interaction. Linguistic anthropology has not, to date, fulfilled the promise of mid-century ordinary language philosophy and the bold proposals put forth by Austin and Wittgenstein – and indeed before them by Malinowski – on the basis of fieldwork in the Trobriands. In particular, we propose that theories of semiotic effectiveness, as illuminating as they may be, do not distinguish action from effect, illocution from perlocution, purpose from consequence. We are not arguing for a simplistic revival of intentional action and autonomous, rational actors, but we do insist that (A) people have goals and plans, and (B) the intuitive guiding assumption that people act in accordance with their goals and plans is fundamental for human sociality.

A telling example is to be found in the case of Rosaldo, whose 1982 article 'The Things We Do with Words: Ilongot Speech Acts' is now a classic of linguistic anthropology and played an important role in the development of the field. Rosaldo challenged the speech act theory of John Searle and particularly his emphasis on the act of promising. Ilongot people, she argued, don't really go in for promises. Rather the prototypical speech act for Ilongots is the command (*tuydek*). Whereas the promise presupposes a particular kind of person/agent who acts sincerely to commit himself to some future course of action (cf. Nietzsche [1997] 1967), the command indexically presupposes and entails a different set of relations between speaker and recipient and possible others. In its own way, each command recreates the social world.

The reader may object: even if linguistic anthropologists have not consistently and rigorously distinguished between action and effect, is it really that important? How important is the notion of purposive action to our understanding of the social world? Our response would be this: purposive action is absolutely central to our understanding of social life. Running through social life are multiple, intersecting lines of purposive action which dynamically give it temporal and sequential structure and, at the same time, provide for a distinctive form of human intersubjectivity upon which we build all the institutional structures, from kinship to kingship, from politics to aesthetics, with which we are surrounded. These are the elements of collective intentionality. Purposive action, whether it be individually or jointly pursued, provides the ever-unfolding, emergent yet structured context within which social life has meaning. From a child's plea to be fed to an octogenarian's request to die, from a declaration of war to a waiter's offer of water – social life is essentially action, and participating in social life is about interpreting others' behaviour as purposive action, and in turn inviting others to interpret our behaviour as purposive action.

The view developed in this book is in many ways closer to the heirs of Malinowski than it is to mainstream linguistic anthropology. Here we have in mind students of ritual such as Leach (1968), Tambiah (1979), Finnegan (1969), and especially Rappaport (1999) who adopted and adapted many of Malinowski's insights and combined them with the speech act theory of Austin.

Basic Problems for a Theory of Action in Interaction

Two basic problems confront the theory of action in interaction. The first is the problem of description, which poses the question: what is involved in saying that someone 'X-ed'? Among the most influential attempts to address this question are those of, *inter alia*,

Aristotle (see Ackrill (1978), Austin (1962), Wittgenstein (1953), and Anscombe (1957)). Anscombe, a scholar of Aristotle and a student of Wittgenstein, articulates, in her *Intention*, the culmination of this tradition. We will briefly consider her argument below as it relates to an account of action in interaction.

The second problem poses the question: what is involved in producing an appropriate response to what someone said or did? In comparison to the first question this one has received relatively little attention from philosophers though it is a more basic and fundamental issue. It is our contention in this book that most attempts to address this issue have seen it as derivative of the first problem. That is, it has been assumed, though rarely stated explicitly, that in order to respond appropriately to some prior action one first has to arrive at a formulation or description of that action. We will not only suggest that this is not correct, we will propose that it is backwards in the following way: to describe or formulate an action is itself just one, rather special, kind of possible response (it is to respond with a representational interpretant in Peirce's sense; see Kockelman 2005, 2013; Enfield 2013). One first needs to know how one might rightfully respond to an action before one can attempt to say what that action is.[2]

What accounts for the conceptual muddle that characterizes much of the scholarly thinking in this area? We believe that it is a consequence of the reflexive character of language combined with the underlying, purposive, goal-directed, intentional nature of human social interaction. Humans are goal-directed creatures who relentlessly pursue manifold purposes through the medium of social interaction. At the same time we are self-reflexive and endowed with a semiotic apparatus in the form of language that is capable of, and indeed largely built upon, subtle forms of reflexivity. Language

---

[2] Our point should be reminiscent of the classic reversal in research on the psychology of emotion: It is not that we run because we are scared; rather, we say we are scared because we find ourselves running!

appears to be the only system of communication that can be used to communicate not only about the sender, and the world around the sender, but also about the communicative system itself. The result is that people are continuously engaged in forms of reflexive talk. A major resource for this is the vocabulary of so-called speech act verbs or *verba dicendi*. The categories that these verbs embody have been more or less completely naturalized and have infected scholarly thinking about language to the point that it is well-nigh impossible to engage in scholarly discourse without employing them.

But it is a demonstrable fact that a rightful response to an action does not require formulation or description of that action, as we discuss in detail in Chapter 4 and elsewhere in this book. To preview that discussion, consider a scene at a dinner table. Dinner is finished and the host has risen from her chair and is circling the table. As she approaches a guest, she extends her arm and opens her hand into a 'receiving' handshape. The guest passes the plate that is in front of him. The host takes it into the kitchen. What has happened? What action did the host perform? Specifically, was this 'a request' (for the guest to pass the plate) or 'an offer' (to clear away his dishes)?

Of course many different kinds of answer have been proposed to such questions. One answer would make reference to the host's inner intention; another would focus on the guest's interpretation. But both of these answers are based entirely on speculation about unobservable inner events and therefore on events that could not possibly have had any consequence for the public organization of action in interaction.

We can see quite clearly in a case like this that the two problems that we introduced above are quite distinct. These participants might end up bringing the action of the host 'under a description'. If they do, as Anscombe pointed out, some of these may be as intentional and some unintentional. For instance, if the host is described as 'offering to clear the dishes' or 'requesting the guest to pass his plate', the action so described is intentional. If, instead, the host is described as 'displacing the air' or as 'moving her hand across another participant's line of sight' or as 'making a gesture that reminded the guest of his recently deceased mother', in all likelihood what is described is unintentional, though no less accurate or true.

We can see plainly from this example that once the guest is able to discern what the host wants – i.e., her intention, purpose, goal, desire that the table be cleared – it is possible to produce a response with no further formulation or description of what she is doing. Responses, then, seem to be built not in relation to described or formulated actions per se but in relation to possible understandings of the intention, purpose, or goal of the other.

What happens if, in our scene at the dinner table, we add some words? How does this change our understanding of what is going on? For instance, what if, as she extends her hand, the host says, *Can you pass me your plate please?* and the recipient responds with *Of course* as the plate is handed over? Or, alternatively, what if the host says *May I take your plate?* and the guest *Yes, thanks?* In the first case we can perhaps say, with some confidence, that the host performed a request, and in the second an offer. The verbal accompaniment to the very same bodily behaviour (which was after all sufficient for the purpose without that verbal accompaniment) seems to tip us off as to what is going on. Importantly, there is still no formulation or description of what is being done, no naming of the action, either in the doing or in the responding. But at the same time, the example seems to suggest that action description or formulation is immanent, if inexplicit, in the doing of action with words. That is to say, part of what we are doing in using words such as these is indexing possible action descriptions or formulations of our actions.

We propose that what is going on here is more a matter of accountability than of ontology. The point is central to our argument in this book. The issue is not what a speaker has done, but what a speaker can be rightly held to account by others for having done. This includes – in the classic sense from Garfinkel (1967) – not just what can be noticed but what can be *reported* in what a person does. Such 'reports', which constitute the kind of social talk that makes up the vast majority of what people say (cf. Dunbar 1996), can be made anywhere on a continuum from explicit, on-record evaluations, on the one hand, to the subtlest of hints, on the other (Grice 1989).

Be that as it may, all the host had to do to get the plate was extend her arm and make a particular shape with her hand, one that would be recognizable to a recipient as preparatory to receiving the plate. Action in interaction is in these ways self-explicating and accountable. Participants need not say, in so many words, what they are doing because others are ready to infer something from the evidence available. Thus, action in interaction always occupies that space between just doing, on the one hand, and saying what one is doing, on the other. The modes of self-explication are not uniform – a diverse range of considerations are always at play, a 'motley' in Wittgensteinian terms: 'I should like to say: mathematics is a *motley* of techniques of proof. – And upon this is based its manifold applicability and its importance' (Wittgenstein [1956] 1978, III, §46, our emphasis).

Of course 'saying what I am currently doing' does not in any way guarantee that I am in fact doing that action. People often say such things as *I bet it's nice* without thereby performing the action of betting. The reason that such sayings do not come off as 'bettings' or 'wagers' has nothing to do with any failure to meet felicity conditions (of, for instance, being in a position to bet, etc.; Austin 1962). If we consider some examples from recorded telephone conversations, we see the speech act verb *to bet* being used in the first-person, present, indicative (thus conforming to what is routinely described as an explicit performative), but in none of them is the speaker treated by the recipient's response as having 'made a bet' (that could be accepted and so on):[3]

(1) NB IV, 10 –

```
01   Emma:        Oh isn' that wonder[ful]
02   Lottie:                       [h h]Jeeziz Chrise shu sh'd
03                see that house E(h)mma yih'av no idea.
04                h[hmhh
05   Emma: →       [I bet it's a drea:m.<Wih the swimming POO:L
06                ENCLO:SED[HU:H?
07   Lottie:               [u- Oh:::::::: Kho:d we .hhihhh uh hu
08
09                -We swam in the n:ude .hh Sundee night u(h)ntil
10                aba[ht  ]two u]h'clo]:ck.
11   Emma:        [ehh]h e h ]h e h]huh h a:h ha[:<
12   Lottie:                                    [HUH
```

(2) NB IV, 10 –

```
01   Lottie:      we swam (.)-a:ll day dihday I d -I never: (.) well
02                I got out abaht e'ry (.) five minutes er so
03                e[n then]'n ]take] a ]
04   Emma: →       [°Oh I°]bet]cher]TA]:nned.
05                (0.2)
06   Lottie:      .hh -YA:H. Kin'a yea:h.=
07   Emma:        =Mm hm:,
08   Lottie:      .hhh En the:n: (.) ah lef' there e(.)t uh:: (0.7) ts -
09                exa:c'ly et three o'clo:ck.
10   Emma:        .pt.hhhh
```

(3) NB:II:3:R

```
01   Lottie:      . . . lo:,
02   Emma:        G'morning Letitia= ((smile voice))
03   Lottie:      =u.-hHow'r YOU:.=
04   Emma:        =FI:NE HOW'R [YOU:.
05   Lottie:                   [eh he:h heh WUDIYIH kno:w.=
```

---

[3] Examples from conversation are presented using the transcription conventions first developed by Gail Jefferson (see Jefferson 2013; see also Sidnell 2009a for a relatively complete recent glossary as well as some discussion of the application of these conventions to languages other than English). It is important to note that in this system punctuation marks intonation and not syntax.

```
06   Emma:        =.hhh Jis got down last ni:ght.eh
07   Lottie:      OH YOU DI[:D?
08   Emma:                   ['hhh We BEEN tuh PA:LM
09                SPRI:NGS.
10                (0.2)
11   Lottie:→     Oh: God ah bet it's [ho:[:t.
12   Emma:                            [.hh[hunderd'n fiftee:n.h
13                (0.2)
14   Lottie:      Oh:::.go::sh.
```

People in interaction don't need to name actions in order to perform
them. And as we see in these examples, even in cases where they do
in fact name an action (e.g., 'bet') they often turn out to be doing
something else (see also *I promise*, which often accompanies a threat
rather than a promise). There is, then, a considerable gulf between
the action described and the action accomplished. Clearly there are
connections, but these are complex and multiple. How we are to
understand this relation is one of the central problems that we
address in this book.

The Evidence from Practices of Repair

For a unique lens on the problem of action, we can turn to the phenomenon of conversational repair, the set of practices used for dealing with
problems of speaking, hearing, and understanding (Schegloff, Jefferson,
and Sacks 1977; Hayashi, Raymond, and Sidnell 2013). Repair is useful
for present purposes precisely because it is a means whereby people can
use language to direct attention to language itself, in the interests of
dealing with 'troubles' with language, including troubles with the understanding of an action that a person is trying to perform with a given
utterance.

It might be objected that so far we have considered only those cases in
which everything runs off smoothly, cases, that is, in which participants'
assumptions about what the other is doing need not be articulated as

descriptions or formulations. Perhaps it is only when trouble arises with the recognition or evaluation of actions that participants will be forced to make explicit the descriptions or formulations that are otherwise tacit in order to put the common focus of attention on the action just at hand. Again, while there are certainly occasions of trouble in which participants name or formulate what they or some other party was doing, this is by no means always the case. Indeed, the first line of defence against troubles of action ascription does not seem to involve formulation at all.

Consider, for instance, cases in which a speaker's first go at an action leaves the recipient uncertain as to what is intended. A common way to deal with such uncertainty is to initiate repair with an 'open repair initiator' such as *What?*, *Huh?* or *Pardon?* and this prompts a redoing of the action such that what is being done will become recognizable to the recipient (see Drew 1997). Consider the following example from a telephone conversation between friends Pyatt and Bush.

```
(4) Pyatt and Bush TC II(b):#28
25   Bush:    I sure haven't seen Leo but- (1.0) I was gonna call
26            him yesterday an tell him to come over here.=
27   Pyatt:   =Yeh.
28            (0.2)
29            Well I guess I'll jus sit back an wait for
30            somebody to call me and tell me [that-
31   Bush:                                    [Yeah he'll
32            probably call you [(in the )
33   Pyatt:                     [Hell I don't know what desert
34            he's in,
35            (0.5)
36   Bush:    Huh?
37   Pyatt:   u- u- I don't know. He says "diyou know where he
38            might be." Well- (0.2) I don't know what desert he's
39            in.
40   Bush:    Yeah,
41   Pyatt:   I don't whether he went to S::- to the Sahara desert,
42            the Mohave, the-
```

Pyatt has called Bush to ask him if he knows where a mutual acquaintance Leo might be (i.e., if Bush has heard from Leo). Bush has indicated that he doesn't know the whereabouts of the person in question and the talk has turned to other things. At the point where the transcript begins, Bush is returning to the matter of what Pyatt has called about. Pyatt responds by saying, 'Well I guess I'll jus sit back an wait for somebody to call me and tell me', thereby apparently resigning himself to the fact that he will not be able to locate Leo. This thought triggers for him a complaint: why should he be able to locate Leo? His first attempt to convey this in lines 33–4 is marked as a complaint by the inclusion of 'Hell', but Bush apparently has difficulty with understanding this, and initiates repair at line 36.

Pyatt's complaint hinges on the fact that he has been asked where Leo might be by Leo's brother. A question such as this implies (1) that Pyatt might know or be in a position to find out where Leo is and, (2) that he has some responsibility to keep track of Leo's movements (and perhaps even to 'look out for him'). It is this implication which Pyatt apparently finds objectionable and which forms the basis of his complaint in lines 33–4. Thus 'Hell I don't know what desert he's in' challenges the presumption of the question to which it was originally produced as a response (whether Pyatt actually said this or simply thought it we cannot tell). As a report to Bush, it is a complaint about being asked a question which holds Pyatt accountable for knowing Leo's whereabouts. The repair at lines 37–9 makes this context available to Bush.

Notice, then, that nowhere in this talk do the participants resort to explicit descriptions or formulations of the actions that have been attempted but are not being successfully interpreted. On the contrary, the talk is self-explicating in the sense we have discussed above. Where there are problems of understanding, this is dealt with by providing more of the details which provide for that self-explication and not by saying in so many words what is being done.

Now, interestingly in this case, Pyatt does formulate what someone else did. In line 37 Pyatt reports 'He says ... ', thereby describing or formulating (in a rather vague way let it be noted) what someone else did. And there are, of course, cases in which such formulations are used to deal with problems related to the recognition of action. Consider, for instance, the following case, taken from an American talk show, in which host Ellen DeGeneres says to guest Rashida Jones 'How great is that?' in speaking about Jones's current television project *Parks and Recreation*.

(5) Rashida Jones on Ellen 04, 2009
```
01  DeGen:  Al:right tell people about this hilarious show.
02          It's Parks and Recreation an' you an' Amy
03          Poehler how- How great is that.=
04  Jones:  =It's pretty great=
05  DeGen:  =mm mh[m.
06  Jones:        [It's- uhm- it- I just mean it- ek-
07          experientially for me it's pr(h)etty
08          [gr(h)ea(h)t(h) [heh heh ha (  )
09  DeGen:  [yeah.          [no. an' but I mean it's
10          a- I ah- know what you mea[nt. But I: say
11  Jones:                           [hih huh ha hah ha
12          [huh huh .hh hah
13  DeGen:  [it's really great. The two of you.=
14  Jones:  nyeah.
15  DeGen:  yeah. [an' it's about,
16  Jones:       [(it is)
```

The final, and sequentially most relevant, part of the turn at lines 01–03 is ambiguous. 'How great is that' can be heard in at least one of two ways: first, as a real information question, i.e., a request for Jones to specify how great that is, and second, as an idiomatic expression that, by virtue of the presupposition it carries, conveys 'That's great!'. To shorthand and simplify this with heuristic action labels (see Chapter 4 on the problems involved), we can say that 'How great is that' can be heard either as an 'information request' or as an 'assessment', and given Jones's involvement, a 'compliment'. Jones's response appears to treat the talk as an information question by specifying the degree (pretty great) that DeGeneres asked about (how great). But while DeGeneres is apparently prepared to accept this as an adequate response, as soon as she has said it Jones orients to an alternate possible hearing of what she has said; not an answer to a question but rather an agreement to an assessment/ compliment.

In accordance with the norm against self-praise (see Pomerantz 1978; Sidnell 2010a), this prompts Jones to produce a string of self-repairs in lines 06–08 the effect of which is to cast herself as a beneficiary (rather than the agent) of that which DeGeneres has complimented (Jones says, in effect, 'I just mean experientially for me it's pretty great', thus downplaying a possible reading of self-praise: 'What I did was great'). Through an interesting turn of events, this sequence has thus resulted in Jones first saying something that could sound like an act of self-praise, and second having to guard against such a hearing through successive modifications via self-repair. In an effort to remedy this awkward situation, DeGeneres then produces a third position repair of her talk in line 03 (see Schegloff 1992; Sidnell 2010a, 2014; Raymond and Sidnell 2014). Specifically, with 'no. an' but I mean', DeGeneres rejects the understanding of her own earlier talk (in line 03) that Jones's response has displayed while with 'I know what you meant' she suggests that Jones's self-repair was unnecessary.

With the final part of this turn at lines 10–13, DeGeneres redoes the action, insisting that 'I say it's really great' thereby (with 'I' and 'say') clarifying that her intended action was to compliment Jones rather than to ask for her opinion. But note that even though she explicitly names her earlier action in drawing attention to it and clarifying what she had meant it to be, she uses a very broad description: 'say' rather than 'give a compliment'. Even in a case such as this, in which the participants themselves orient to the possibility that what they are doing may be potentially ambiguous and invite unwarranted inferences, they seldom resort to the use of fine-grained action labels such as 'compliment' (at least, not with reference to the current speech event itself; such action labels are more often used to describe events that are remote from the current speech event and participants, as in 'She was complimenting me on my latest TV show'). Instead, DeGeneres seeks to clarify what she was doing using the most general descriptive terms available ('say') and by rejecting the understanding that Jones has displayed.

Let us, finally, note the following. We do not deny the possibility of a person saying something like *I was complimenting you*, thus using a fine-grained description of their own action in meta-semiotic fashion, but this is clearly a last resort, and it is indeed interactionally poor form; trying to clarify what you had meant to do is not only an acknowledgement of your own failure to formulate an action properly and of the other person's failure to interpret it properly, but worse, it is an acknowledgement of a failure of the relationship between interlocutors (cf. Enfield 2013: Chapter 13).

We may conclude by suggesting that even in cases where there is a problem of action ascription or understanding – where what the speaker means to be doing is not clear – the participants need not resort to formulation, and, indeed, in many cases it is not clear that doing so is either useful or even possible.

Practices and Actions, Orchestrations and Inferences

We are proposing that the central problem within linguistic pragmatics, linguistic anthropology, and other neighbouring fields of study concerns how saying something can count as doing something. We have further suggested that this can be broken down into two more specific questions; the problem of accurate description and the problem of appropriate response.

Much of the work in this area has drawn on the ideas of John Searle and others who have argued for a solution to the problem based on a theory of speech acts. While there are different versions of the theory, a common assumption seems to be that actions are relatively discrete and can be classified or categorized. Applied to interaction, the theory suggests that recipients listen for cues (or clues) that allow for the identification of whatever act the talk is meant to be doing (greeting, complaining, requesting, inviting). Moreover, the theory seems to presume a closed set or inventory of actions that are cued by a delimited range of linguistic devices. On this view, the basic problem to be accounted for by scholars of interaction is how participants are able so quickly to ascribe an action interpretation to what is being done (see Levinson 2012).

It is well known that participants in interaction are able to respond to prior turns with no waiting, no gap, and so on (indeed they often respond in slight overlap). Operating with the standard assumptions of psycholinguistics (i.e., that speech recognition and language comprehension require processing time, that speech production requires planning time and so on), this creates something of a mystery: how are participants able not only to parse the turn-at-talk into turn-constructional units (TCUs) (and thereby anticipate points of possible completion) but also to recognize what action is being done in and through those units and somehow be prepared to respond to that action with little or no latency (indeed, in cases of overlapped response, with less than zero latency)?

Speech act theory, applied to interaction, attempts to solve this problem by adopting what we describe as a binning approach, wherein recipients of talk are thought of as sorting the stream of interactional conduct into appropriate bins or categories (see Chapter 4). The alternative account which we develop in this book treats action as, always, a contextualized and token construal of some configuration of practices in interaction. For the most part, explicit labellings or formulations of actions (whether done consciously or not) are not necessary to insure the orderly flow of interaction. All that is necessary is appropriate response. Participants respond on the fly and infer what a speaker is doing from a broad range of evidence. However, on occasion (such as in some cases of reported speech and in some cases of third position repair) a speaker formulates, using the vernacular metalinguistic terms available to her, the action that she or another participant is understood to have accomplished (e.g., *I requested that he get off the table!, I'm not asking you to come down, I'm just saying you're welcome if you want*, etc.). And, of course, in various kinds of *post hoc* reporting contexts and in scholarly analysis, people outside of an interaction often label or formulate the actions that appear to have been done. So an alternative to the binning or speech act account is one in which producing an 'action' (in quotation marks to indicate that this is merely a heuristic use of the word) involves putting together, configuring, or orchestrating a range of distinct practices of conduct to allow others to infer that the speaker is doing 'x' or 'y' where 'x' or 'y' are possible formulations or descriptions.

It is often suggested by conversation analysts that there is no necessary one-to-one mapping between a given practice of speaking (e.g., *do you want me to come over and get her?*) and some specific action (such as an 'offer'), and this is usually meant to suggest a many-to-one relation running in both directions: i.e., there are multiple ways/practices/methods to accomplish any given action, and any given practice can, in context, be understood to accomplish a range of different actions (see, e.g., Schegloff 1997; Sidnell 2010a; Enfield 2013). While this is no doubt true (in so far as the terms in which it formulates the problem are adequate, e.g., 'context', 'an action'), matters are a good deal more complicated, since any determination of 'what a speaker is doing' is an inference from a complex putting together of distinct practices – of composition, context, and positioning.

Levinson (2012), puzzling as to how recipients are seemingly able to determine so quickly what action is being done and then somehow respond without delay, distinguishes two major types of information that can be gleaned from a turn-at-talk. On the one hand, there is the 'front-loaded' information of prosody (e.g., pitch reset at the beginning of a TCU), gaze direction, and turn-initial tokens (such as *oh, look, well,* and so on) that can potentially tip off a recipient as to what is being done. On the other hand, there is the detailed linguistic information which is only revealed as the turn-at-talk unfolds. This includes much of the information available through grammatical formatting (e.g., morphosyntactic inversion, imperative marking, semantically rich discourse particles, etc.) as well as through richly informative linguistic formulations (e.g., *the deal, my boss, stupid trial thing,* etc; see (6), below). While Levinson thus recognizes that the passage from a turn-at-talk to 'an action' involves a recipient putting together various strands of evidence, he argues that the solution must involve a delimited inventory of actions, recognition of which these practices, solely or in combination, are able to trigger. Alternatively, we argue that the 'inference from a complex set of features' model implies an inevitable degree of indeterminacy in action ascription which is always merely a provisional inference from evidence.

It is well established in conversation analysis (Sidnell 2010a; Sidnell and Stivers 2012) that one can look to subsequent turns in order to find evidence for an analysis of previous turns – this is called the 'next turn proof procedure'[4] (Sacks et al. 1974; see Chapter 4 below for further discussion). In the analysis of single cases, we can ground our analysis of some turn as, for instance, an 'accusation' by looking to see how

---

[4] Importantly, it is not technically a proof procedure but rather a possible disproof procedure: the 'proof' referred to here is in fact no more than a failure to disprove, which is in line with the idea that analyses (by both analysts and participants) of others' behaviour are always only provisional (Enfield 2013:88).

a recipient responded to it (e.g., with an excuse or justification). Sacks et al. (1974) proposed along these lines that

> while understandings of other turns' talk are displayed to co-participants, they are available as well to professional analysts, who are thereby afforded a proof criterion . . . for the analysis of what a turn's talk is occupied with. Since it is the parties' understandings of prior turns' talk that is relevant to their construction of next turns, it is THEIR understandings that are wanted for analysis. The display of those understandings in the talk of subsequent turns affords both a resource for the analysis of prior turns and a proof procedure for professional analyses of prior turns – resources intrinsic to the data themselves.

This data-internal evidence is used, for instance, to ground the claim that when Debbie says 'what is the deal' in line 15 of example (6) below, she is not simply asking a question but is, in doing so, accusing Shelley of wrong-doing:

(6) Debbie and Shelley
```
12   Shelley:   distric attorneys office.
13   Debbie:    Shelley:?,
14   Shelley:   Debbie?,=
15   Debbie:    ^what is tha dea::l.
16   Shelley:   whadayou ^mean.
17   Debbie:    yuh not gonna go::?
18              (0.2)
19   Shelley:   well -hh now: my boss wants me to go: an: uhm
20              finish this >stupid< trial thing, u[hm
```

'What is the deal' is hearable as an accusation, i.e., as conveying that Shelley has done or is otherwise responsible for something that Debbie is unhappy about. What aspects of the talk convey this? First, the positioning of the question, pre-empting 'how are you' type inquiries at this early stage of the call, provides for a hearing of this as abrupt and in some sense interruptive of the usual niceties with which a call's opening is typically occupied (e.g., *How are you?*). Second, by posing a question which requires Shelley to figure out what is meant by 'the deal', Debbie thereby suggests that Shelley should already know what she is talking about and thus that there is something in the common ground, something to which both Debbie and Shelley are already attending (or have on their minds). Third, by selecting the idiom 'the deal' to index this thing in the common ground, Debbie reveals her stance towards what she is talking about as 'a problem' or as something that she is not happy about, etc. Fourth, with the prosody, including the stress on 'is' so that it is not contracted, the emphasis on 'dea::l.' and the apparent pitch reset with which the turn begins, Debbie conveys heightened emotional involvement. Putting all this together, we can hear in what Debbie says here something other than a simple request for information: instead it is something like a complaint or accusation. Debbie is clearly upset and the implication is that Shelley is responsible. But how can we ground the analysis of the turn in question in the displayed orientations of the participants themselves? To do this we look to Shelley's response.

That Shelley hears in this more than a simple question is evidenced first by her plea of innocence with 'whadayou ^mean.' and secondly by her excuse. All other-initiations of repair indicate that the speaker has encountered a trouble of hearing or understanding in the previous turn. Among these, 'What do you mean' appears specifically adapted to indicate a problem of understanding based on presuppositions about common ground (Raymond and Sidnell nd). Here 'what do you mean?', which is produced with a noticeably higher pitch, suggests Shelley does not understand what Debbie means by the clearly allusive, in-the-know expression, 'the deal'. More narrowly, it conveys that the expression 'what is the deal' has asked Shelley to search for a possible problem that she is perhaps responsible for, and that no such problem can be identified. It is thus hearable as claiming 'innocence'.

When Debbie redoes the question, in response to the initiation of repair by 'What do you mean', she does it with a yes–no (polar) question that strongly suggests she already knows the answer. 'You're not going to go' is what Pomerantz (1988) called a candidate answer question that presents, in a declarative format, to Shelley what Debbie suspects is the answer and merely requests confirmation. This, then, reveals the problem that Debbie had in mind and meant to refer to by 'the deal'.

And when Shelley responds to the repaired question, she does so with what is recognizable as an excuse. This is a 'type non-conforming' response (i.e., one that contains no 'yes' or 'no' token; see Raymond 2003) in which Shelley pushes the responsibility for not going (which is implied, not stated) onto 'her boss' (invoking the undeniable obligations of work in the district attorney's office) and suggesting that the obstacle here is an inconvenience for *her* (as well as for Debbie) by characterizing the impediment to her participation as a 'stupid trial-thing'.

Clearly, as the quote from Sacks et al. (1974) makes clear and as the foregoing discussion is meant to explicate, the most important data-internal evidence for the meaning or import of the utterance in line 15 we have comes in *subsequent talk*. In the case we have considered, subsequent talk reveals how Shelley herself understood the talk that has been addressed to her. This understanding is embodied in her way of responding.

It is important to clarify exactly what is being claimed. Subsequent talk, and data-internal evidence, allows us to ground the analysis of this utterance – 'What is the deal' – as projecting a possible complaint or accusation of Shelley by Debbie. It does not, however, tell us what specific features of the talk cue, convey, or carry that complaint/accusation. As the pioneers of conversation analysis demonstrated, in order to address *that* question, the question as to which specific features or practices provide for an understanding of what a given turn is doing, we need to look across different cases. We need to isolate these features in order to discern their generic, context-free, cohort-independent character (Garfinkel and Sacks 1970). So case-by-case analysis (single case analysis using data-internal evidence) inevitably leaves us with a question – specifically, what particular aspects of a turn convey (or allow for an inference about) what the speaker is doing (i.e., what 'action' is being done)? What are the particular practices of speaking that result in that consequence? And, inversely, what are the generic features of any practice that are independent of this particular context, situation, group of participants, etc.?

In order to attempt an answer to these questions, we have to move beyond the analysis of a single case to look at multiple instances. However, and this is the key point in the context of the present discussion, when we do this we inevitably find that each practice which is put together with others in some particular instance (to effect some particular action outcome) can be used in other ways, combined with other practices, to result in other outcomes. We can take any particular feature or practice from the Debbie and Shelley case and work out from there. We can look in new materials for questions that, like Debbie's *What is the deal?*, occur in this position, pre-empting what normatively happens in the opening turns of a telephone call. If we do this we find that some are like this one and seem to deliver or imply what might be called an accusation, but others do not. We can look at other cases in which a speaker refers to something as *the deal* or asks *What is the deal?* and again find some cases in which something like a complaint or accusation is inferred, but others in which it is not. And we can find other instances in which similar prosody is used in the formation of a question or instances in which something like a question is delivered with an initial pitch reset. The result is always the same: no single feature is associated with some particular action outcome. The conclusion we must then draw is that 'action' is an inference from a diverse set of evidences that a speaker puts together, or orchestrates within a single TCU or utterance (see also Robinson 2007).

Language, Action, and Accountability

An implication of what we have so far said is that talk-in-interaction provides for a distinctive form of human intersubjectivity, one that builds upon specific properties of human language including reference, semanticity, discreteness, reflexivity, and reportability (see Hockett 1960; Sidnell 2014). The very fact that a linguistic utterance can be repeated and/or reported provides for a special kind of accountability that is unique in the animal world. Anything you say can be used as evidence – whether for or against you. So we can think of linguistically mediated social interaction as a dynamic unfolding of social relations, between speaker and hearer, storyteller and audience, and so on. On this view, the relevant types of social relations are made manifest only through particular uses of language.

There is another way in which to think of this language-society dependency. As anthropologists such as Evans-Pritchard (1937), Malinowski (1935), and Gluckman (1963) among others point out, specific verbal activities, uses of language – such as gossip, cross-examination, lecturing, and praise-singing – support and underwrite particular social relations and structures at higher levels. Azande social relations are partially built upon a set of practices for making accusations, for consulting an oracle, and so on (Evans-Pritchard 1937). Gossip, as described by Gluckman and others, includes practices for referring to, commenting upon, and evaluating aspects of conduct and thereby serves to activate the tyranny of accountability through which social relations are constituted. Social relations among the Nuer, and anywhere else that anthropologists have studied, are supported by specific forms of address and self-reference (Sidnell and Shohet 2013). Further examples abound.

Much of human social reality (and all of what Searle calls institutional reality) is constituted through language, but perhaps more importantly all of it rests upon a foundation of talk. A key idea here is normative accountability. Searle proposes a notion of deontic powers, characterized as 'rights, duties, obligations, requirements, permissions, authorizations, entitlements, and so on' (Searle 2010:9). The key mechanism that sustains these powers is that 'once recognized, they provide us with reasons for acting that are independent of our inclinations and desires' (ibid.). We are then potentially subject to others' evaluation and appraisal of our behaviour in terms of how well it conforms with those 'reasons for acting'. This idea gets at only one aspect of accountability. For whatever institutionally defined status a speaker (or hearer) may inhabit, there are norms or expectations that govern it, which means that a person's actions *as president* (or mother, or professor, or vegan, etc.) can be discussed and evaluated as good, bad, fitting, inappropriate, adequate, problematic, and so on, given the set of rights and duties that defines the status in question (Enfield 2013; Kockelman 2013). That is, the whole edifice and logical structure of institutional reality that Searle describes is supported by talk about that edifice.

Our point is this. The mechanism by which rights and duties are defined and maintained is a linguistic mechanism. Language is what gives us the capacity to thematize or put common focus on another's behaviour, *as a behaviour – or 'action' – of a given type* and then express surprise, sanction, approval, or any other evaluative stance about that behaviour. This is why language is so integral to both action (and thus, power) and accountability in human social life.

It is important to understand the breadth of this account. The relevant statuses that define normative accountability in institutionalized social relations run the gamut from permanent and long-term statuses (husband, Dutch, etc.) to more transitory statuses (acquaintance, friend, close friend), to highly fleeting but still normatively and morally binding statuses such as being 'the one who has just been asked a question'. Any person who inhabits a status, at any of these scales, must orient to the possibility, indeed probability, that their conduct as an incumbent of that status will be evaluated, assessed, critiqued, commended, praised, etc. Thus, accountability exerts both a projective and a retrospective force. People feel its power both as an effect of conduct, after the fact, and in their anticipation of such effects, before the fact. One manifestation of this is seen in speakers' explicit accounting for their behaviour (using language). Consider when a speaker says, for instance, *Need more ice* as she gets up from the table and thus exits momentarily from the conversation taking place (Goodwin 1987). By saying 'Need more ice', she is accounting for her departure and thereby encouraging others not to read into her conduct unwanted inferences, e.g., that she was insulted, bored, or embarrassed by what was just said.[5] The feared negative implications are constantly possible products of the 'web of inferences' that a person is never free from and never has the luxury of disregarding. This is what we mean by the tyranny of accountability. As Garfinkel warned, people will always find a way to interpret our behaviour as having reasons behind it, whether we like it or not.

Language is central in all this. As we have noted, among the unique properties of language are reference (directly linking the message to things in the context by creating joint attention on those things, and adopting some descriptive or evaluative stance towards those things) and displacement (the possibility of referring to things, events, and people that are not present in the here and now of the speech situation). These two properties, combined with the reflexivity of language – the capacity of the communicative system to be used to refer to itself – allow for the description and, through this, public assessment of linguistic practice and other conduct. Only with these features can I use language to draw attention to what you said or did earlier on, and say new things

---

[5] There is evidence that this sort of thing is a widespread practice across cultures. In a video-recorded interaction between speakers of Kri, a speaker gets up in the middle of a conversation to leave the scene, and in doing so says *sɔm bang dɔɔjq* meaning 'Just going to boil some bamboo shoots' (050801a_06.40), thus volunteering an account for her otherwise unexplained departure.

about those communicative behaviours, for example expressing opinions as to their appropriateness or effectiveness.

Our view of the classic core design features of language is that they are about social accountability and social action, not (just) about the representation of information. These same properties are what make it possible to 'narrate' one's own conduct (e.g., saying 'Need more ice' as one leaves the table to account for one's departure and mark it as temporary) in such a way as to guide its interpretation by others, and thus to account for it.

Examples like this show that language is a tool of accountability. But crucially, language is also often the *object* of accountability. Just as we may narrate what is being done in order to allow others to make sense of it, so we may narrate what is *said*: hence, the utility of our linguistic resources for describing speech acts, and thus for casting a single speech event in different ways (cf. He **told** *me about that, He* **complained** *to me about that, He* **informed** *me of that*). So, conduct accomplished through language – in a word, *talk* – has properties that make it the object of a special kind of accountability (and flexibility, to invoke the other side of the coin of agency). Features that Hockett described as discreteness and semanticity (which, when understood within a relational totality, Saussure described in terms of *identity*) allow utterances to be repeated and reported, and thus make them available as targets for accountability. Moreover, as Austin noted, linguistic acts are decomposable in special ways by virtue of their specifically linguistic character, and as such can be talked about in ways that are at least more difficult, if not impossible, for other forms of conduct. Thus, we can describe the way someone gestured but not its referential meaning or locutionary force. The reflexive, meta-semiotic features of language and talk thus open up unique possibilities for highly complex forms of social accountability and, as a result, for richer and more sophisticated social processes than anything else known in the animal world.

This line of thinking allows for an important reconceptualization of Malinowski's key insights into the role of language in social life, expressed in the following passage from Malinowski's masterpiece of intuitive linguistics, *Coral Gardens and Their Magic* (1935:7):

(T)here is nothing more dangerous than to imagine that language is a process running parallel and exactly corresponding to mental process, and that the function of language is to reflect or to duplicate the mental reality of man in a secondary flow of verbal equivalents ... The fact is that the main function of language is not to express thought, not to duplicate mental processes, but rather to play an active, pragmatic part in human behavior. Thus in its primary function it is one of the chief cultural forces and an adjunct to bodily activities. Indeed, it is an indispensable ingredient of all concerted human action.

Malinowski's key insight is that language is as much a mode of action as it is an instrument of reflection. The concept of accountability allows us to see how this is the case. Language is not just an instrument of action but simultaneously the means by which persons make what they are doing, and *why* they are doing it, intelligible to others. That is to say, language provides the means by which action in interaction can appear as properly motivated, reasonable, rational, in a word, accountable. Where some such aspect of conduct is not in this sense intelligible, language provides the means by which it can be questioned and queried and so on. This is the hurly-burly of conduct of which Wittgenstein spoke. The complex web of accountability that contextualizes a bit of conduct is the very stuff of action – indeed, in some cases, such as when someone acts by simply withholding a response, it is all there is!

The remarkable and important propositional (i.e., referential, predicational) function of language – its capacity to serve as a symbolic system that purports to reflect a world out there – has often been treated as the locus of human culture in language whether in the form of narratives, accounts provided in response to an interviewer's question, or as a structure that replicates or manifests culture in its purest form. But in fact this is what makes language unique with respect to all other human capacities (see Silverstein 1976; and see, in particular, Jakobson's 1990a and 1990b seminal statements). If we want to understand language as a part of culture, Malinowski suggests, we need to see it for what it is – a vehicle of action in the sociocultural world.

Actions, Accountability, Outcomes

Consider an example, in which friends Janet and Ann are talking on the phone. In the course of the call, Janet, speaking of her daughter who is at Ann's house, says, *Do you want me to come and get her?* This is understood, by Ann, to implement an offer rather than as merely asking about her wants. So here then a practice of speaking in context conveys some recognizable action which achieves an interactional goal. In such a situation, the speaker is understood as accountable for having done whatever action is so effected. Thus, Janet is accountable (primarily) for having made an offer, rather than for having asked something. Accountability is realized in various ways. For instance, a next speaker produces a turn that treats the previous speaker as having done the action for which this turn is an appropriately fitted response (e.g., next speaker produces an acceptance to an offer rather than an answer to a question). In the example, Ann eventually accepts Janet's offer. Alternatively, or simultaneously, a next speaker may explicitly name the action they understand the first speaker to have done saying, for instance, *thank you for offering*.

So by making it recognizable to a recipient what action(s) one intends to accomplish, a speaker thereby becomes accountable for having done that action. But it is sometimes desirable to achieve some particular outcome while evading the accountability that attaches to the doing of the action that typically results in it. How is this done? We give three examples.

Getting a Caller's Name by Simply Giving One's Own Name

Sacks (1995) noted that in calls to a suicide prevention hotline requests for the caller's name were often met with suspicious resistance and questions such as 'Why do you need to know?' To avoid this, call-takers would first introduce themselves as, e.g., 'Mr. Jones', thereby eliciting reciprocal name-identifications without being on record as having asked for this information. Sacks notes that if a staff member asks 'Would you give me your name?' the caller can ask 'Why?'. Sacks (1995: 4) notes, 'What one does with "Why?" is to propose about some action that it is an "accountable action".' Saying 'This is Mr. Jones, may I help you?' may be a way of getting the other person to provide her name, but it is not an accountable action in that respect; one cannot say in response 'Why do you want my name?' because the name was never asked for.

Fishing for Information by Telling 'My-Side'

Pomerantz (1980, following Sacks 1995) described a strategy of 'my-side telling', in which one participant merely tells of their limited access to some state of affairs, thereby eliciting information about it without having to ask explicitly. In a particularly well-known case, Emma says 'Yer line's been busy', conveying her 'limited access' to events which the recipient knows about. This prompts Nancy to provide information about how it was that her phone was busy, who she was talking to, and why she was talking for such an extended period. Emma succeeds in getting information without having to ask for it and thus without having to do something that might be characterizable as 'nosey' or similar. Given that actions are accountable, a person should not ask a question unless they are entitled to ask it and, moreover, have a good reason for doing so. When people respond with *Why do you ask?* or even *It's none of your business*, this relates to the accountability of actions, as do reports about a person being a *gossip, a nosey parker*, or *a busybody*, etc. With this in mind, we can see how the practice Pomerantz describes might have important interactional uses: using this practice, a person may achieve the action of eliciting information about some specific state of affairs, yet without being accountable for having asked a question.

Eliciting an Offer by Describing a Trouble

In a final set of cases, rather than make a request, a speaker merely describes a trouble, thereby inviting the other to offer what seems to be wanted (see, for discussion, Pomerantz and Heritage 2012). If the offer is not made or is not sufficient, the speaker can then upgrade, that is, 'go on record' and make the request. In one instance a landlady (Alice) is talking to her tenant: she establishes that the tenant is using a laundry machine in her basement apartment, and then she reports the problem that she now has 'no water' in her own home. When the tenant offers a solution that would merely fix the immediate problem (by shutting it off), Alice ends up going on record with the requesting action, saying 'Well I don't want you to shut it off mid-load, just don't run it anymore.'

And in another case, Donny, who has called his friend Marcia, incrementally builds up a description of his predicament saying 'Guess what', 'My car is stalled', 'I'm up here in the Glen', etc. When this does not elicit an offer from Marcia, Donny seems to be on the verge of formulating a request ('I don't know if it's possible') but instead continues with a telling of his trouble. At this point Marcia interjects, indicating that she has understood what Donny wants and that, if it were possible, she would comply (see Schegloff 1995).

Across these and many other examples, we see that a simple troubles-telling can prompt from the recipient an offer of help, or at least an account for not producing such an offer. In this way, a speaker can achieve the outcome of getting another person to do something without being accountable for having actually imposed in this way.

Conclusion

Our examples show that people are acutely aware of the account-ability that attaches to the actions they are recognized as doing. In certain circumstances they seek to avoid that accountability by achieving their interactional goals through alternate means. Speakers can bypass the action/recognition node of the [practice] → [action/recognition] → [interactional goal] chain such that they are able to mobilize the agency of another without being accountable for having done so. The action's outcome is achieved yet the action itself is ostensibly not done.

When speakers implement actions in 'on record' ways, using prac-tices that are designed to be recognizably and 'officially' implementing those actions, they will thus be accountable for having done the actions in question. People may then ask why this action is being done, or they can report to others that the action has been done, glossing it in some specific way (*She asked if I was going, She complained that it was too hot*). Obviously, formulations of prior actions can be challenged or contested, but that does not change the underlying fact that participants become accountable for the actions that they are recognized as having done. It is therefore not surprising that people often aim to achieve interactional outcomes or goals without being accountable for having done the actions that would normally effect these.

Part II

The Nature of Action

THREE

The Distribution of Action

If actions are what constitute social relations in enchrony, and therefore ultimately the fabric of our social groups, this implies a central role for agents, that is, those who carry out actions (Kockelman 2007a; Enfield 2013; Enfield and Kockelman 2017). Who are agents and what is the nature of their agency?

(1) Agents have *flexibility* over meaningful behaviour, in so far as:

a. to some degree they *control* or determine that the behaviour is done at a certain place and time;

b. to some degree they *compose* or design the behaviour as a means for a particular end; a thing to be done and a way to do it;

c. to some degree they *subprehend*[1] or anticipate how others could view and react to the behaviour; for instance, to some extent they may be prepared for certain interpretants – i.e., rational responses – by others; they may be surprised or disposed to sanction non-anticipated interpretants.

With an agent's flexibility comes accountability:

(2) Agents have *accountability* for meaningful behaviour, in so far as:

a. they may be subject to public *evaluation* by others for their behaviour, where this evaluation – in the form of interpretants like praise, blame, or

---

[1] *Subprehend* may be defined as follows. If you subprehend something, it is as if you anticipate or expect it, but not in any active or conscious way; rather, if you subprehend something, when it happens you cannot say later that you had not anticipated or expected it. Subprehension is thus close to the notion of *habitus* (Bourdieu 1977).

demand for reasons – may focus on any of the distinct components of flexibility given in (1), above;

b. they may be regarded as having some degree of *entitlement* to carry out the behaviour, and give reasons for it, and they or others may invoke this entitlement; this may relate to any of the distinct components of flexibility given in (1), above.

c. they may be regarded by others as having some degree of *obligation* to carry out the behaviour, and give reasons for it, and they or others may invoke this obligation; this may relate to any of the distinct components of flexibility laid out in (1), above.

To summarize it, as Kockelman (2007a) might: agency equals flexibility plus accountability. How flexible you are depends on how freely you can determine the elements of a course of behaviour and its outcomes, in multiple senses: the physical carrying out of the behaviour, the planning, design, and execution of the behaviour, the placing of the behaviour in an appropriate context, the anticipation or subprehension of likely effects of the behaviour – including, especially, the reactions of others – in that context. How accountable you are depends on how much it can be expected or demanded that other people will interpret what you do in certain ways, e.g., by responding, asking for reasons, sanctioning, praising, or blaming you. With these elements distinguished, we begin to understand why the concept of agency is far from simple or primitive, and why it has resisted easy definition (see Enfield and Kockelman 2017).

The Case of Recruitments

Now it is easy to think that 'an agent' should coincide exactly with an individual. But this is seldom the case. When Bill gets John to open the door, it is Bill who plans the behaviour but John who executes it. Or when Mary reports what a professor said in yesterday's lecture, it is Mary who speaks the words but the professor who is accountable for what was expressed. With distributed agency, multiple people act as one, sharing or sharing out the elements of agency. One man commits a misdeed against another, and yet revenge is taken years later between the two men's grandchildren, neither of whom was involved in the original transgression. When someone is held to account for something that someone else chose to do, agency, with its components of flexibility and accountability, is divided and shared out among multiple individuals. Agents do not equal individuals: the locus of agency is the social unit, and social units are not defined by individual bodies.

In the rest of this chapter, we discuss some of the elements of human sociality that serve as the social and cognitive infrastructure or preconditions for the use of recruitments in interaction.[2] The notion of an agent with goals is a canonical starting point, though importantly agency tends not to be wholly located in individuals but, rather, is socially distributed (Enfield and Kockelman 2017). This is well illustrated in the case of request-like actions, in which the person or group that has a certain goal is not necessarily the one who carries out the behaviour towards that goal. In the remainder of this chapter, we focus on the role of semiotic (mostly linguistic) resources in negotiating the distribution of agency with request-like actions, with examples from video-recorded interaction in Lao, a language spoken in Laos and nearby countries. The examples illustrate five hallmarks of requesting in human interaction, which show some ways in which our 'manipulation' of other people is quite unlike our manipulation of tools: (1) that even though B is being manipulated, B wants to help; (2) that while A is manipulating B now, A may be manipulated in return later; (3) that the goal of the behaviour may be

---

[2] 'Recruitments' encompass all instances of conduct by Person A that occasion assistance from Person B (see discussion in the present chapter, and Floyd, Rossi, and Enfield in press). Our discussion of recruitments, requests, joint action, cooperation, and distributed agency owes much to the collective input of research collaborators in the Human Sociality and Systems of Language Use project (MPI Nijmegen 2010–2014): see Enfield 2011, 2014b, Rossi 2012, 2014, 2015, Floyd et al 2014, Kendrick and Drew 2016, Rossi and Zinken 2016, Enfield and Kockelman 2017.

shared between A and B; (4) that B may not comply, or may comply otherwise than as requested because of actual or potential contingencies; and (5) that A and B are accountable to one another: reasons may be asked for, and/or given, for the request. These hallmarks of requesting are grounded in a prosocial framework of human agency.

Flexibility in the Pursuit of Goals

In the opening pages of his *Principles of Psychology*, William James (1890) notes the special flexibility of cognizant behaviour. Iron filings, he notes, will be drawn to a magnet, but they cannot choose how they reach that goal. If a paper card covers the magnet, the filings will just press against the card. Thinking beings are different:

Romeo wants Juliet as the filings want the magnet; and if no obstacles intervene he moves towards her by as straight a line as they. But Romeo and Juliet, if a wall be built between them, do not remain idiotically pressing their faces against its opposite sides like the magnet and the filings with the card. Romeo soon finds a circuitous way, by scaling a wall or otherwise, of touching Juliet's lips directly.

(James 1890:7)

This means–ends flexibility is our forte. We try to reach a goal, and if this is frustrated, we seek or invent new means. 'The pursuance of future ends and the choice of means for their attainment are thus the mark and criterion of the presence of mentality' (James 1890:8). A certain mentality is always involved in the pursuit of goals, but that is not our point of interest here. We want to focus on what results from this mentality: namely, our enhanced flexibility in selecting means to ends.

To see how we refine and elaborate our choices of means for ends, just look at the instruments and tools of human technologies (cf. Zipf 1949; Suchman 1987; Lave 1988; Norman 1988; Clark 2007). But possibly our most important, and most ancient, means towards ends are *other people*.

Rather than doing everything ourselves, or even doing things just with the help of tools, it is often other people that we use to help us reach our goals.

This should not be taken to mean that people are solely interested in exploiting others for our own ends. Situations in which one person uses another as a tool are not based in selfishness alone. One reason is that we are apparently just as willing to offer *ourselves* as tools to serve *others'* individual goals. We hold doors open for strangers. We alert people when we notice they have dropped their keys. We give away our spare change on the street. We open doors for people when we see their hands are full. Another reason is that we *share* goals with others. So, when I behave in a way that looks like it's *for you*, it may in fact be *for us*. Tomasello (2008) argues that this is the mechanism whereby altruistic behaviour can evolve in a selfish world. Once individuals are able to share a goal, a behaviour that is *for us* is thereby, ultimately, also *for me*.

Language as a Tool for Mobilizing Others

We do not manipulate people in the same direct way that we grasp a hammer or a pen. If we are going to get others to do things for us, we need the mediating tools of communication. As Bloomfield (1933) put it, when a stimulus evokes a response (e.g., when Jane sees an apple on a tree and wants to pluck it), language can be used as a sort of tool of transference, to elicit that response in another person (she tells Jack that the apple is there, and asks him to pluck it for her). We influence other people by taking the tools provided by our language and culture and using them to persuade those other people to willingly act on our behalf. This is the essence of what we are doing when we make requests. Our speech acts have deontic powers: with speech acts we bestow our reasons for action onto other people.

Humans have by far the most complex communication systems of all creatures. Our languages are generative in nature, meaning that we can combine words and constructions to produce entirely novel utterances at will. These verbal utterances may be further creatively combined with accompanying visible bodily behaviour. We shall use the term *language+* (pronounced 'language plus') to refer to the enriched set of semiotic resources that includes not just words and grammatical constructions but intonation, gestures, facial expressions, and more (Kendon 2004; McNeill 2005; Enfield 2009).

Now while the set of semiotic means we have for getting others to do things is, in principle, infinite, in fact we often use recurring and readily recognized strategies in making requests (**Could you** *pass the salt?*, **Could you** *open the window?* **Could you** *shut the door?*). We now consider some of the types of strategies that recur in a single language community. The following cases are taken from video-recordings of conversation among speakers of Lao, the national language of Laos (Enfield 2007a, 2013). Here are three simple examples of ways in which people use language to get others to do things for them, or to help them, in Lao.

In the first example, two women are in a kitchen, where one of the women needs some leaf extract that the other has been preparing. The first woman says 'grab (it and) come (here)', meaning 'bring it here':

(3) INTCN_030731b_192570_0:03:13

01	A:	qaw3 maa2
		grab come
		Bring it here (referring to a bowl of leaf extract)

| 02 | B: | ((Slides bowl with extract in direction of A)) |

In this case, the requester uses a stripped-back linguistic construction that does nothing more than refer directly to the action being requested. The action – to fetch something –is idiomatically expressed in Lao as a combination of 'grab' and 'come'. The object being referred to – the leaf extract – is understood from the context.

A second example shows the common strategy in Lao of adding a 'softening' sentence-final imperative particle *nὲὲɪ* to the basic action being requested (see Enfield 2007a:66 and *passim* for description of a paradigm of particles whose meanings code imperative illocutionary force). In addition, the speaker makes a pointing gesture in the direction of the thing she is asking for:

(4) INTCN_030731b_196430_0:03:16

```
01   A:   qaw3     qanø-nii4    nὲὲɪ
          grab     CLF-this     IMP.SOFT
          Grab this thing (for me)
          ((referring to prepared food in a sieve; Pointing
          in direction of the food that she is asking B to pass))
```

```
02   B:   ((Turns to reach out for the food, grabs it and passes it to A))
```

In a third case, the speaker is busy with food preparation in the kitchen. She uses a circuitous or indirect strategy, with more embellishment of the basic request being made than we saw in the last two examples. She addresses the requestee explicitly (calling him 'father' – he is her father), and rather than stating the action she wants him to carry out (i.e., pass her the knife), she asks whether the knife is behind him:

(5) CONV_020723b_RCR_970010_0:16:10

```
01   A:   phòòɪ    miit4   thaang2     lang3    caw4       mii2    bòò3
          father   knife   direction   back     2SG.POL    have    QPLR
          Dad is there a knife behind you?
```

```
02   B:   nii4  nii4
          here  here
          Here, here
          ((Finds a knife behind himself,
          passes it towards A))
```

It is clear that she doesn't simply want to know whether there is a knife behind him. The question makes sense in terms of her current goals. She is asking because she wants the knife, and so he hands it to her.

Now look at what these three cases have in common. Person A wants to get hold of some entity that is nearby but out of reach. Rather than go and get it herself, Person A says something to Person B, with the result that Person B gets the thing and passes it, thus carrying out a bit of behaviour that Person A would otherwise have had to carry out herself.

Such moves as those shown in the 'A' lines of the above examples are not always about a requester getting a requestee to act physically in her stead. Sometimes the issue is getting 'permission'. In the next example, a girl wants to use the knife that her older brother is holding and playing with. She leans over to take it out of his hand (illustrated in Figure 3.1;

Figure 3.1 Video still coinciding with line 1 in example (3). Girl, A, leans over to take knife out of older brother's, B, hand.

A and B in the foreground of the shot). Just when her hand comes close enough to take the knife herself, she produces an imperative construction identical in form to the one shown in (3), above:

(6) INTCN_030731b_730407_0:12:10

01   A: qaw3   maa2
            grab   come
            Bring it here ((pulls knife out of B's hand))

02   B: ((Allows A to take knife that B is playing with))

The requestee's response here is not to do anything at all, but merely to allow the requester to take control of the object in his hand.

Here is another case (illustrated in Figures 3.2a, b). The requestee, B, is visible at the left of frame in Figures 3.2a, wearing a T-shirt. She is

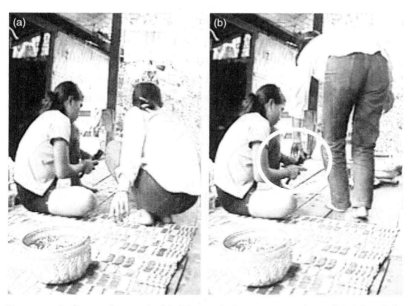

Figure 3.2 In line 1 of example (7) (Fig. 3.2a), the requester, A, to the right of the frame, reaches down to take the knife out of B's hand. In line 2 (Fig. 3.2b), B allows A to take the knife.

holding a knife and playing with it, using it to whittle away at some piece of stem or similar object. The requester, A, to the right of the frame, reaches down to take the knife out of B's hand, and as she does so, she issues a less elliptical version of the request in (6), saying not just 'grab and bring (it here)' but more explicitly 'grab the knife and bring it here to give me':

(7) INTCN_030731b_0:11:43

01 A: qaw3   miit4   maa2   haj5   khòòj5
        grab   knife   come   give   1SG.POL
        Give the knife to me
        ((pulls knife out of B's hand))

02 B: ((Allows A to take knife))

Again, the effect of the words that A uses is not to get B to act in any way, but rather to allow A to take the knife out of B's hand, which A immediately does.

Notice that the linguistic construction of this last example contrasts with the request in (3) in two ways. First, there is explicit mention of the object that is being requested. It is not clear why this is being added (similarly with the addition of reference to the object as 'this thing' in (4)). Second, the requestee is explicit that the request is 'for' her. A possible motivation for this addition of self-reference is that it allows the speaker to select from among a set of personal pronouns, here choosing a more polite form than she would normally use for this addressee, presumably helping to 'soften' the request.

These examples give us a simple look at the kind of role that language plays in manipulating the behaviour of others in order to get them to contribute to, or comply with, our own goals. The examples show that different formulations are possible. And they show that such cases are not only about getting others to act on our behalf, but possibly also about getting others to desist from some behaviour that then allows us to proceed with our goal. Either way, B complies with a low-cost imposition.

The request-like cases we have just considered reveal a defining feature of human sociality, namely the distributed nature of our agency (see above, and Enfield 2013:115 and *passim*; see also Kockelman 2013; Gell 1998). This is related to the notion of distributed cognition, familiar from research by authors such as Goody (1977), Suchman (1987), Lave (1988), Norman (1988), Hutchins (1995, 2006), and Clark (2007), who have all shown ways in which tools and artefacts can be extensions of the human body and mind (see also Enfield 2009, Chapter 6). Students of language have long argued that language is a kind of tool for getting others to do things. Some, including Zipf (1949), have gone further, saying that *other people* are tools for us as well (see also Goodwin 2006 on this point in relation to language). Along these lines, Pagel (2012:275–6) has recently compared language to a remote control device: 'When you speak, you are using a form of telemetry, not so different from the remote control of your television ... Just as we use the infrared device to alter some electronic setting within a television so that it tunes to a different channel that suits our mood, we use our language to alter the settings inside someone else's brain in a way that will serve our interests.'

Sometimes it appears as if this were really true. In the following example, one person uses speech to get another person to turn the television on, just as she might otherwise have used a remote control device to do from a distance:

(8) INTCN_111204t_818990_0:13:39

01   A: peet5   tholathatı bengı mèè4
           open   television look   IMP.UNIMP
           Turn on the television (for us) to watch

02   B: peet5   bòø   daj4   tii4
           open   NEG   can   QPLR.PRESM
           It doesn't work (it can't be turned on), I think

03 A: daj4 - caw4   kaø   peet5 bengı thaø   mèè4
        can   2SG.POL   TLNK   open   look   PCL   IMP.UNIMP
        Yes it works - you turn it on and see

04 B: ((Moves towards the television and reaches
        and switches it on.))

Then half a minute later:

(9) INTCN_111204t_850175_0:14:10

01 A: mòòt4   mòòt4   laø   mèè4
        turn.off turn.off PRF   IMP.UNIMP
        Switch it off, switch it off.

02 B: ((Moves towards the television and reaches
        and switches it off.))

It is an inviting analogy: asking someone to do something for us is like pressing buttons on a remote control device. But like all analogies (as Pagel of course knows), it is imperfect. As we shall now see, its imperfections are instructive. The following sections consider the ways in which the analogy between words and remote control devices breaks down.

Hallmarks of Recruiting

What is the difference between using a person and using a device as a means to get something done? The answer: with people, both parties are goal-driven and socially accountable beings, and there is a social relationship between them. Here are some features of the interpersonal manipulations shown in the above examples that are not observed in the use of an electronic remote control device:

1. Even though B is being manipulated, B wants to help.
2. While A is manipulating B now, A may be manipulated in return later.

3. The goal of the behaviour may be shared between A and B.
4. B may not comply, or may comply otherwise than as requested because of actual or potential contingencies.
5. A and B are accountable to one another; reasons may be asked for, and/or given.

There are of course other differences. But these will serve as points of focus for us to consider the hallmarks of recruiting in humans, within the simple framework of goal-directed social agency outlined in the above sections.

B Wants to Do the Recruited Action

A remote control device is a robot. It responds to instruction, but it doesn't offer to help you or otherwise independently anticipate your needs. People, by contrast, may want to help. Think about the above examples. In no case would we want to say that someone was being coerced or seriously imposed upon. The requestees cooperate without any resistance or comment. People are so willing to help that we often see them offer assistance without their having to be asked.

Consider an illustration of the kind of situation in which a person needs something to be done for them and gets the help they need from another person without having to ask for it or otherwise signal the need. Figure 3.3 shows a panel of three stills from a video recording, taken in quick succession. Our focus is the man in the white T-shirt seated in the background at the left of the image as we view it. This recording is taken in the kitchen verandah of a Lao village house. The floor of this space is raised high above the ground of the village compound. To get up into the house, one walks up a steep galley-style ladder. The man in the white T-shirt is sitting where one of these ladders provides entry onto the raised floor of the house. The area

Figure 3.3 A man holding a large basket (bottom right in Fig. 3.3a) reaches a half-closed gate, which another man pushes open for him (Fig. 3.3b) so that he can walk through (Fig. 3.3c).

where the ladder provides entry onto the floor is blocked by a low gate, designed to prevent toddlers from falling down the ladder. In Figure 3.3a, the leftmost panel, we see that the gate is ajar, just in front of the man in the white T-shirt. While the gate is not completely closed, it is closed enough so as to hinder entry for somebody who does not have a free hand with which to open the gate. At the moment illustrated in Figure 3.3a, another man is at the bottom of the ladder, about to go up into the house. This man is just visible (though partly obscured by the banister) in the bottom right corner of the image, with two stripes across his T-shirt. He is holding a large plastic laundry basket full of clothes, which he is about to bring up into the house. Figure 3.3b shows the point at which he is reaching the half-closed gate at the top of the ladder, and where one can thus foresee that his way may be hindered. It is at this moment, as can be seen in Figure 3.3b, that the man in the white T-shirt reaches forward with his right hand and pushes the gate open enough to allow the other man to walk up into the house unhindered. In Figure 3.3c, we see the silhouette of the man with the large laundry basket walking through the now-open gate and onto the raised floor of the house.

(10) INTCN_111203l_243630_0:04:04

01   A: ((begins walking up ladder approaching closed gate with washing basket in hand, Fig. 3.3a))

02   B: ((reaches out to gate as A comes to top of ladder, Fig. 3.3b, and pushes open gate for A to walk through unhindered, Fig. 3.3c.))

This is not a request sequence; rather, it can be seen as an instance of the more general action of recruitment: a sequence in which a first move by A occasions a helping action by B. As in request sequences (see the above examples), A's behaviour makes it clear that he needs help, and then B helps accordingly, in line with a general cooperative stance in human interaction. But in this case A's behaviour, which makes it clear that he needs help, cannot be said to have been an intentional manipulation of B to help A in achieving his goal. Here, person B stepped in to help A upon anticipating a potential problem. The point here is that request sequences all presuppose the more general prosocial, cooperative orientation and desire to help that is sometimes simply volunteered in cases like this one.

Roles May Be Reversed

In the kinds of social contexts we spend most time in – i.e., informal social interaction in familiar environments with people we know well – the kinds of things we ask others to do are the kinds of things we are willing to do for them. I expect you to pass me the salt when I ask, just as when you ask for the salt, you can expect that I will pass it. Obviously there are asymmetries, especially when interactions are more formalized, but the general principle is reciprocity. This is obviously not the case with remote control devices.

The Goal May Be Shared

The cases we have considered so far involve situations in which person B is asked to help person A with something related to their current goal. But many things that we might want to call requests or similar occur in contexts where both people involved are jointly committed to the same goal. Rossi (2012) compares two kinds of request sequence in Italian interaction. In one kind, A has a goal, not currently shared with B, and asks B to help (e.g., 'Pass me the chewing gum'). In another kind, A and B currently share an overarching goal, and A asks B to do something that they have effectively already committed to within that overarching goal (e.g., 'Deal the cards'). The idea of joint commitment, and everything that implies (Clark 2006), is clearly irrelevant to the relationship between people and remote control devices.

The fact that people make joint commitments to goals means that, similar to the 'gate at the top of the ladder' example above (example (10)), cooperation can be assumed and may be offered without having been prompted. And when there are shared goals, it can become impossible – and in fact irrelevant – to say whether a sequence involved a request or an offer.

In the following example, we are interested in the two people at the back of the image (most clearly visible in Figure 3.4b, the man standing stooped over, the woman with her left hand on her head). They are cooking a dish together. The man has been heating jugged fish on the fire, and at this moment the jugged fish needs to be strained. In Figure 3.4a, the man (crouched down at the left back of image, but

Figure 3.4 The man at the left back of the image has a pot of heated fish and he is getting another pot, into which to strain it (Fig. 3.4a); the woman at back right extends her arm forward with the sieve in her hand; the man walks over, holds the empty pot underneath the sieve, and pours the jugged fish into the sieve (Fig. 3.4b).

mostly obscured) has just emerged from the fireplace with the pot of heated jugged fish, and he is getting another pot, into which to strain it. Seeing this, the woman at the back of the image on our right extends her arm forward with the sieve that she has in her hand (see the centre of the image in Figure 3.4a). Next, the man walks over, holds the empty pot underneath the sieve, and pours the jugged fish into the sieve, thus straining it.

(11) INTCN_030731b_267220_0:04:27

01   A: ((Holds out sieve for straining jugged fish, Fig. 3.4a))

02   B: ((Brings and places jugged fish and pot for jugged fish to be strained into, Fig. 3.4b.))

In this instance we can't say whether this sequence involves an offer or a request (nor do we need to; see above, and next chapter). The terms *offer* and *request* presuppose that the relevant behaviour is 'for' one or the other of the two parties. If A offers to do something, it's *for* B. If A requests that B does something, it's *for* A. But in many cases like this one, the behaviour being precipitated is a sub-part of a routine to which both parties are already committed, and thus share as a goal.

B Need Not Comply

If a piece of technology is in working order, it will do what you want. A person, on the other hand, may ignore your request, refuse to comply, or do something other than what you asked. The lives of people are full of contingencies, actual or potential, which often intervene (cf. Curl and Drew 2008).

In the following example, a husband and wife are in a kitchen, skinning catfish. They have been doing this for a while, and the husband has one more fish left to skin but complains that his back is sore from sitting and working. He holds the fish out towards his wife for her to take and skin:

(12) INTCN_111203l_689141_0:11:29

```
01   A:   cêp2   qèèw3   lèèw4
          hurt   back    PRF
          My back hurts

02        bùt2   diaw3
          a moment
          (It will only take) a moment

03        qaw3   qaw2
          grab   grab
          Here take it
          ((holding out fish for her to take))

04   B:   mm2
          nope
          No.
```

Her refusal is not surprising. The couple, who in this culture are of equal standing in a setting like this one, have each been working for the same amount of time doing the same task. The wife's back is no doubt also sore from sitting and working, and she treats the request as unwarranted. There's no good reason why she should do it for him.

While the B speaker did not give a reason for her refusal in the last example, often a reason is given, or at least implied. In the next example, two sisters are involved in preparations for lunch. One of the dishes they will eat is green papaya salad. They have already prepared the papaya by julienning it, and it is now ready to be pounded along with various other ingredients to make the salad. Speaker A asks Speaker B to go and get the mortar and pound the salad. Normally, this salad is eaten immediately after it has been pounded and tossed, and so it is too early to proceed, since various other dishes are not yet ready. Speaker B does not comply with A's request, instead saying 'Don't rush':

(13) INTCN_030731b_695170_0:11:35

01	A:	paj3	qaw3	khok1	maø	tam3	paj2
		go	grab	mortar	come	pound	IMP.GO

Go and get a mortar to do the pounding

02	B:	qoo4	jaa1	faaw4	thòòq2
		Oh	don't	rush	PCL

Oh, don't rush.

Speaker B is not declining to do the requested behaviour. She is declining to do it at the moment asked. By effectively giving a reason for not complying, she makes it clear that she is not simply being uncooperative.

One May Need to Give B Reasons Why They Should Do the Action

A remote control device never needs or wants to know why you want it to do something on your behalf, but a person often does.

The Distribution of Action

We saw in the last section that people who are asked to do things may give reasons for refusal or delay in complying. Here we shall see that people who ask others to do things will sometimes give reasons as well. (We saw a case where the man reasoned that because his back hurt, his wife should finish his task.) This happens, for example, when a person is asked to do something but delays their response, or otherwise resists. Giving a reason for a request is a way to pursue, strengthen, or help make sense of what is being asked.

Let us look at an example. Here, Speaker A starts by issuing a directive to a group of three people (two are her children, one is her daughter-in-law) who are preparing food in the kitchen of her house. She asks them to toss the rice. This is a procedure in the preparation of glutinous rice. When rice has been steamed and is now cooked, because of the shape of the steamer used it will be cooked more in some spots and less in others. Tossing the rice is a way of evening out the texture of it before serving:

(14) INTCN_111203l_425170_0:07:05

01 A: suaj3 khaw5 mèè4   suu3
        toss rice IMP.UNIMP   2PL.BARE
        Toss the rice you lot

She uses the second-person plural pronoun *suu3* in formulating this request. This means that she does not select any one person to do the job. As it happens, none of the three young people in her immediate vicinity volunteer to act upon her request. It is clear that they are fully occupied with other duties. She then calls out to a fourth person – her son-in-law whose name is *Nyao* – to come and do it instead. At this moment, Nyao is away from the scene, doing something else in the compound outside the house, but within earshot. Her move (shown in (15)) begins with a somewhat elaborate request in line 1: she selects him explicitly by name, telling him to stop what he is currently doing and to come and toss the rice, adding also that it's 'for her'; she also uses the imperative sentence-final particle *mèè4*, which implies that the addressee is 'unimpeded' (often implying 'Why aren't you already doing it?'; cf. Enfield 2007a:63), and she immediately adds two reasons, the first, why it has to be done, and fast ('the pot will burn'), and second why *he* has to be the one to do it ('the others are all busy here'):

(15) INTCN_111203l_427440_0:07:07

01 A: bak2-ñaaw2 paq2   vaj4 han5 maa2 suaj3 khaw5
        M.BARE-Ñ abandon put   there come toss rice
        Nyao, drop that and come and toss the rice

02   haj5 kuu3   mèè4
        give 1SG.BARE IMP.UNIMP
        for me

03   maj5 mòò5 dêj2   niø khaw3   khaa2 viak4
        burn pot FAC.INFORM TPC 3PL.BARE stuck work
        the pot will burn - they are busy

        met2 thuk1 khon2 niø
        all every person TPC
        all of them

04 B: ((Stops what he's doing and walks up the ladder
        into the food preparation area, goes into the kitchen
        to toss the rice. It takes 13 seconds before he reaches
        the kitchen))

Note that Nyao would otherwise not have been expected to be involved in the behaviour of tossing the rice, since he was, relative to four other people including the speaker, the furthest from the place where the task needed to be done. It is by providing explicit reasons that Speaker A in (15) is able to mobilize his help. In this way, we see language clearly serving as a tool for creating deontic powers: specifically, for transferring reasons for acting onto other people.

The drawing of attention to a reason for acting alone has long been recognized as an indirect way of requesting (cf. *'It's cold in here'* as a way of getting someone to close the window; see previous chapter). Here is a case in which Speaker A draws attention to a problem that needs attending to, namely the fact that some live fish in a pot don't have sufficient water to keep them alive and fresh:

(16) INTCN_111203l_601081_0:10:01

```
01   A:   paa3   man2   siø     bòø    taaj3   vaa3
          fish   3.B    IRR    NEG    die     QPLR.INFER
          The fish, aren't they going to die,

          qaaj4   dong3
          eB      Dong
          Dong?
          ((Pointing in direction of large pot with live fish))

02   B:   qanø-daj3 (.)  qoo4  qaw3  nam4  maa2  saj1 ( )
          what           Oh    grab  water come  put ( )
          What? Oh, put some water in there ( )

          maa2   saj1   mèè4
          come   put    IMP.UNIMP
          put some in
```

It is also often the case that a reason is given in combination with an explicit request. Here is an example, in which an imperative command is followed quickly by a reason. Speaker A is sitting next to a large pot with live fish in the bottom of it. A fresh load of water has just been poured into the pot, and the fish are splashing about so much that water is spilling out of the pot and onto him:

(17) INTCN_111203l_629110_0:10:29

01 A: ñòò4 nii3 (.) man2   diin4 phoot4
         lift   flee   3SG.BARE jump   too.much
         Take it away - they're splashing too much
         ((leaning back from the pot))

02 B: ((Walks around behind A in direction of the pot,
         comes and picks up pot and moves it away.))

By providing a reason for the request to 'take the pot away', Speaker A helps to clarify for B precisely what is being asked of her. There could be a range of reasons why A wants her to take the pot away, and each would imply a different way of complying. For example, how far away should she take it? Here, he makes it clear that he merely wants the pot to be placed far enough away that the splashing water won't reach him.

Conclusion

The concept of agency has long been central to many lines of research that touch on human interaction, in fields ranging from law and sociology to anthropology and linguistics. Importantly, the word 'agency' does not refer to a one-dimensional 'degree of assertiveness' or similar. Its use should reflect the nuances of empirical and theoretical findings of research in this multifaceted and dynamic domain (Kockelman 2007a; Enfield 2013: Chapter 9; cf. Davidson 1963; Duranti 1990, 2004; Gell 1998; Ahearn 2001). Conceptual tools for understanding agency are central to the analysis of any social action, not least requests and their ilk. The behaviour of doing things for others is also supported by a set of psychological and interpersonal resources grounded in human sociality, including the elements of social intelligence, distributed cognition, normative accountability, and cooperative motivations (Enfield and Levinson 2006; Enfield

2013). These resources form part of a foundational infrastructure for social interaction (Levinson 2006; Enfield and Sidnell 2014). Our aim here has been to highlight some hallmarks of recruitment sequences in light of certain defining elements of agency and the infrastructure for interaction. In the sequences we have examined, three of these elements come to the fore.

The first is that we assume that people behave in accordance with goals that they are pursuing. Their behaviour makes sense in terms of those goals and in terms of the reasons that may be given for their behaviour. This is clear in any sequence in which one move occasions cooperative social behaviour in a subsequent move (see Enfield and Kockelman 2017). Second, there is a mismatch between the fact that in the physical realm people are immutably distinct from one another (we have separate bodies), while on the other hand in the realm of social accountability we may be treated either as inhabiting separate units (such as when one person pursues a goal unilaterally) or as being elements of a single, shared unit (such as when two people have made a joint commitment to a shared course of action; cf. Clark 1996; Rossi 2012). Much of social life involves tacking back and forth between different distributions of flexibility and accountability of behaviour, in a process of fission–fusion agency (Enfield 2013:104). Recruitments always imply the sharing or distributing of action. And third, thanks to the special prosociality of our species, we are motivated to help others, and we tend to assume that others have the same cooperative motivations towards us. Recruitments both presuppose and display these mutual prosocial motivations and assumptions.

FOUR

The Ontology of Action

Which actions there are depends on which action concepts figure in people's intentions. We talk about 'taking' an action, as if we were picking an apple from a tree, but actions don't antecedently exist in nature, waiting to be picked. What we call taking an action is actually *making* an action, by *en*acting some act-description or action concept. Which actions we can make depends on which descriptions or concepts are available for us to enact.

(Velleman 2015:27)

Natural Action versus Social Action

By one broad definition, social action is any behaviour that takes another person into account (Parsons 1937; Weber 1947/1961; Anscombe 1957; Davidson 1963, 1978; Giddens 1993; Searle 2010). Weber (1961:173) writes: 'Action is social in so far as, by virtue of the subjective meaning attached to it by the acting individual (or individuals), it takes account of the behavior of others and is thereby oriented in its course.' Weber identifies four types of social action:

(1) Weber's four types of social action
1. Action for *rational ends*: Rational behaviour as means to ends; done for the caused effects of the behaviour; value of this action lies in 'achievement of a result' (to ask 'why' would lead to a clearly statable but perhaps obvious answer).

2. Action for *absolute value*: Acting out of duty, conviction, honour, ritual, etc.
3. Action for *affectual release*: sex, revenge, etc.
4. Action for *mere tradition*: it wouldn't make sense to ask 'why'; there's no answer.

Weber did not motivate these categories from a priori theoretical distinctions,[1] but it might be possible to distinguish the four in terms of their *reasons*:

(2) Weber's four types of social action, framed in terms of different reasons
1. Rational = reason for action is desire to attain the outcome of the behaviour
2. Absolute = reason for action is desire to do (or to have done) the behaviour
3. Affectual = reason for action is desire to experience the behaviour
4. Traditional = reason for action is 'my people do this'

As Weber stresses, these distinctions are far from exclusive. Take sex: having sex is of the rational action type if it is done because the participants want to have a child, while it is of the affectual type if it is done because it feels good (and in certain circumstances, e.g., a loveless marriage, may be 2 or 4). So obviously an action can have roots in multiple, intersecting reasons.

Let us now develop a more focused notion of social action. A social action is a goal-directed swatch of controlled behaviour whose ends are only successfully met by means of someone recognizing that goal and treating the behaviour as a valid means towards the goal.[2] If someone asks *What time is it?*, this swatch of controlled behaviour will count as the action of 'asking the time' when their

---

[1] (Weber 1961:176): 'this classification of the modes of orientation of action is in no sense meant to exhaust the possibilities of the field, but only to formulate in conceptually pure form certain sociologically important types'.

[2] Thus in Ryle's example, a certain eye movement may be a wink or a twitch depending on the recognition of a communicative intention behind it (Geertz 1973:6, with reference to Ryle 1949).

recipient recognizes the practices that contribute to its meaning (presupposing that, among other things, the recipient knows English) and produces a response that is consistent with this recognition, such as providing the time or some other relevant response like *Sorry I don't have a watch.* Or if someone hands over two dollars for their take-away coffee, this swatch of controlled behaviour – physically handing over the money – will count as the action of 'paying for coffee' only as long as the recipient recognizes the practices and contextual factors that contribute to its meaning: the institutional statuses being enacted, the proper exchange value of the currency tokens, and so on. Think of the kinds of things that would be at issue were someone to find themselves having to establish in a court of law that they had, in fact, paid for the coffee.

We can distinguish natural action from social action by acknowledging a fundamental difference in how the outcome or effect of a piece of controlled behaviour is causally realized. In natural action, the outcome is realized by natural causes. I drop a glass; it breaks. Whether or not you make some interpretation of the glass's fall – e.g., you see the glass falling and you wince, figuring it's going to break – this interpretation will have no bearing on the processes that cause the glass to actually break. Your wincing is an interpretant of the glass's falling, in so far as you take the falling to stand – indexically – for the imminent breakage. But the breakage is not an interpretant of the falling. It is simply a result of brute, unmediated natural causes. In social action, by contrast, the ends are realized semiotically: that is, by means of the ascription – by another person – of a meaning to the behaviour, of reasons for the behaviour, and of its goals.

Social action is truly social because its consummation is dependent on another person's subsequent acceptance of its meaning (Searle 2010; see above chapters). This notion of social action is distinct from a more general sense of the term, according to which most controlled human behaviour is in some way shaped by its social relevance and consequences, including how we walk down the street. Our definition of social action is a subset of action in that sense.

Courses of Action

Units of action are not isolated but are conjoined and embedded within larger courses of action. Actions and courses of action can be described at almost any level of granularity. If someone is asked what they are doing, they might reply *Moving my rook to protect my king, Playing chess,* or *Just hanging out,* none of which would be false. Nevertheless, we should expect that there is a privileged basic level of behavioural units – analogous to the privileged 'basic level' of generality in word meaning, *dog* as opposed to *animal* or *kelpie*; Rosch 1978 – such that we recognize that protecting one's king is part of playing chess, but that playing chess is to a lesser extent entailed by or integrated within just hanging out. The way in which we phrase informal proposals in English is sensitive to this kind of distinction. *Let's just hang out* only weakly suggests a commitment to the possibility of playing chess, while *Let's play chess* strongly suggests, if not entails, a commitment to sub-routines like moving one's rook and protecting one's king. And since protecting one's king is an inherent sub-goal of a larger basic-level activity, it would seem odd to phrase an exhortation to protect your king using the same format as a general activity proposal. *Let's play chess* sounds normal, while *Let's protect our kings* sounds odd.[3]

In other words, if someone commits to playing chess, they are committing to moving chess pieces around in certain ways; but if they commit to just hanging out, this is making less of a commitment to playing chess (see Clark 1996, 2006; cf. Levinson 2012 on the notion of

---

[3] It appears that with the *Let's* format, the speaker is trying to secure a joint commitment to the project, while another format might presuppose that a joint commitment to a relevant project is already in place. See Rossi (2012) for an argument along these lines distinguishing between two ways of requesting in Italian. See also Stivers and Sidnell (2016).

higher-level action projects). If they order cigarettes, they have to commit to selecting, or at the very least settling for, a particular brand and not others; if they go to the movies, they commit to this being a particular movie, venue, and time; if they start telling a joke, they commit to delivering a punchline. In these ways, social actions can be dependently incorporated into larger courses of social action. The actions of delivering the punchline or laughing at the joke make sense only in so far as they are incorporated in the larger course of action of participating in the telling of a joke (see Kockelman 2006a on this relation of incorporation in culture more generally).

The Ontology of Action

A central goal of linguistic anthropology is to understand the role that language and associated semiotic systems play in the carrying out of social action, that is, to understand how we pursue our goals, and especially, how we do this in collaboration with others. Any account of social action presupposes an ontology of action whether this is made explicit or not. At one extreme, we might propose that actions have the properties of natural kinds (as implied by Searle 1969, or Levinson 2012, 2016), with clear defining properties and a kind of essential causal basis; analogous to, say, 'citrus fruits'. At the other extreme we might propose that actions are cultural constructions (e.g., Rosaldo 1982; Wierzbicka 2003), roughly comparable across cultures in functional terms but essentially defined by historically developed local practices; analogous to, say, 'desserts' (or 'games' à la Wittgenstein 1953). If social actions are natural kinds, we should be able to count the number of possible actions, in the same way we are able to count types of extant life forms and provide a comprehensive list of all observable actions (difficulties of defining species, etc., notwithstanding). If, on the other hand, actions are cultural constructions, such an exhaustive listing of possible actions could not in principle be done – it would be akin to asking 'How many different kinds of desserts are there?' The difference between citrus fruits and desserts is that we can create new types of dessert for local purposes and according to unique contextual conditions (e.g., availability of ingredients) any time we want. The possibilities are endless.[4]

It seems obvious to us that action realization is subject to *both* universal human contingencies grounded in phylogeny *and* local cultural contingencies that have arisen historically. But we argue that if actions are natural, this is not because they are pre-given or pro-grammed in any sense, but rather because their commonality *emerges*. And if they are culturally constructed, they are still constrained by basic imperatives of social life, and by basic affordances of our bodies and physical settings. Our view, then, is that social actions – such as telling, asking, and requesting – are not natural kinds. They do not spring from innate intentional state categories (as proposed by Searle 2010) or analogous structures. Instead, social actions are the emergent products of dealing with the complex fission–fusion social organization that is characteristic of all human groups (Enfield 2013), and of the need to exercise our flexibility in finding means for pursuing social goals. These are the cognitive, social, and historical conditions that precede, and undergird, the historical emergence of cultural difference.

It is a truism that language is a tool for action, but the theoretical and conceptual issues that follow from this are far from resolved. Our aim in the rest of this chapter is to review the problem of defining and analysing action in interaction, and to propose a solution. In the following section, we deal with three points of conceptual clarification that, we suggest, are indispensible to any discussion of social action and language. We then discuss two case studies that illustrate the core problem of this book: How it is that actions are ascribed (or 'recognized') and thereby con-summated, both by participants in social interaction and by analysts.

---

[4] See Hacking (1998) on 'making up people' for a parallel discussion in relation to kinds of persons.

Three Dimensions of Contrast in the Analysis of Action

Our approach owes partly to Austin and the analytic tradition in philosophy which emphasizes the distinctive properties and importance of intentional or purposive action in contrast to the non-intentional effects of our behaviour. A first point is that both purposive action and non-intentional effects can be seen as ways to do things with words but, as we shall see, they differ in many respects. Second, there is a need to distinguish explicit from primary in action. This distinction is concerned not with the *kind* of action in question, but rather with how it is expressed or formulated. And third, we need to distinguish – as we have already emphasized – between the constitution of action, on the one hand, and the *ex post facto* description of action, on the other. The following subsections deal with these three conceptual points.

Purposive Action versus Effect

If a speaker says to some recipient, *Sir, your lecture today was extremely informative*, they will have paid that recipient a compliment and, in doing so, they will have set in motion a set of relevancies such that the recipient is normatively obliged to respond, and to respond, in some particular way – for instance, with appreciative acceptance (e.g., *Thank you*), with disagreement (e.g., *Not really*), with a turn that redirects the compliment elsewhere (e.g., *I had excellent sources to draw upon*; see Pomerantz 1978). Now, of course, the speaker will have done a whole host of other things in addition to paying the recipient a compliment. For instance, the speaker will have taken a turn, perhaps initiated a larger exchange on the topic of the lecture, perhaps elicited the attention of another person thereby drawing them into a conversation. These we can describe as interactional effects. Moreover, the speaker will have displayed deference to the recipient (by paying him a compliment, and by using the address term *sir*), will have claimed some knowledge of the lecture in question, will have situated the referent being talked about in relation to the current event of speaking. These we can describe as indexical effects, since they are produced by relating, via presupposition or entailment, aspects of the speech signal to particular and recognizable contextual parameters. Finally, in so speaking, the speaker may also have made himself look obsequious, made his recipient feel proud, or made some third party feel awkward.

The distinction between an action and its possible effects has been described in a range of ways: e.g., as a distinction between action and collateral effects (see Chapter 5, below), illocution and perlocution (Austin 1962; Searle 1969), giving and giving off (Goffman 1959:2),[5] pragmatic function$_1$ and pragmatic function$_2$ (Silverstein 1987).[6] Often the distinction between action versus effect correlates with the distinction between what is intended versus what is unintended, but there are exceptions. For instance, a speaker may purposely use a T-form pronoun either to initiate 'familiar' relations or to insult a recipient (see, e.g., Jacquemet 1994). Another example is what Schegloff (2009) refers to as a 'component action'. In the example he gives, a 14-year-old girl named Virginia asks her mother – in a bid for permission to get a job – 'Didn't Beth get to work before she was sixteen'. The mother replies, 'People just don't want *children* waiting on them'. The main line of the mother's purposive action here is clearly an answer to a question and a response to a possible objection (Beth got to work, why can't I?), but by selecting the word 'child' to refer, obliquely, to the recipient, the mother *effects* an insult of Virginia who wants to be considered an adult.

While recognizing such (possible) exceptions, our view is that, in the main, people are engaged in goal-directed purposive action.

---

[5] 'The expressiveness of the individual appears to involve two radically different kinds of sign activity: the expression that he gives, and the expression that he gives off' (Goffman 1959:2).

[6] 'There is a contrasting functionalism that grows out of ancient concerns with rhetoric; it sees function as the purposive, goal-oriented use of speech (or equivalents) by intentional individuals in specific situations of discourse, each such usage constituting a "speech act" or "speech event" (terminologies differ)' (Silverstein 1987:23).

Indeed, this is a fundamental assumption that guides reasoning about others' behaviour. As a result, questions such as *What is he doing?* and *What does she mean?* become omnirelevant. Purposive actions both respond to prior actions and establish relevancies for next actions in such a way as to constitute an architecture of intersubjectivity (as described by Heritage 1984; Sidnell 2014). When people are pursuing such goal-directed actions, they are simultaneously producing effects such as establishing contextual parameters including the presumed social relations between participants, and thereby reproducing aspects of the sociocultural order. As we have noted, it is true that people *can* pursue such effects purposively – e.g., by choosing to address an interlocutor with a T-form or by using French rather than English in a Montreal shop – but they cannot do so without also, at the same time, being understood to accomplish some purposive action of the kind identified with terms such as *request, compliment,* and so on. The framework of normative accountability for what is being done then hangs centrally on what participants in interaction recognize as a *main line* of action (Goffman 1963:43ff.; cf. Kendon 1990; Clark 1996). This has been a central concern of conversation analytic work, and our point here has been well documented within that approach (see, for instance, Schegloff 1968; Schegloff 2007; cf. Levinson 2012).

Explicit versus Primary (cf. 'Implicit' and 'Indirect')

In lecture III of *How to Do Things with Words*, Austin (1962:32) writes the following:

The performative utterances I have taken as examples are all of them highly developed affairs, of the kind that we shall later call explicit performatives, by contrast with merely implicit performatives. That is to say, they (all) begin with or include some highly significant and unambiguous expression such as 'I bet', 'I promise', 'I bequeath' – an expression very commonly also used in naming the act which, in making such an utterance, I am performing – for example betting, promising, bequeathing, &c. But, of course, it is both obvious and important that we can on occasion use the utterance 'go' to achieve practically the same as we achieve by the utterance 'I order you to go': and we should say cheerfully in either case, describing subsequently what someone did, that he ordered me to go ... *Here we have primitive as distinct from explicit performatives*; and there may be nothing in the circumstances by which we can decide whether or not the utterance is performative at all.

(emphasis added)

Austin went on to develop these ideas as the contrast between *explicit* performatives such as 'I promise to be there at 11 o'clock' and *primary* performatives such as 'I'll be there at 11 o'clock'. Austin's point touched on both the hearer's problem of recognition and the speaker's problem of accountability:

If someone says 'I shall be there', we might ask: 'Is that a promise?' We may receive the answer 'Yes', or 'Yes, I promise it' (or 'that ...' or 'to ...'), whereas the answer might have been only : 'No, but I do intend to be' (expressing or announcing an intention), or 'No, but I can foresee that, knowing my weaknesses, I (probably) shall be there'.

(1962:69)

So the difference between an explicit performative and a primary per-formative has to do with what the speaker *may be taken as doing* by another (e.g., a recipient), and, most importantly, what he or she is then *accountable for having done*. In the case of an explicit performative there is, according to Austin, no room for interpretation – the speaker having announced in so many words what they are doing. In the same way that a police uniform leaves little room for doubt as to the set of rights and duties it signifies and bestows, the explicit performative is 'maximally public and minimally ambiguous' (Kockelman 2007b, 2013). In the case of the primary performative, the speaker may be taken as promising or as merely expressing an intention, or alternatively warning the recipient. The key issue then for Austin is about 'making plain what I am doing':[7]

suppose I bow deeply before you; it might not be clear whether I am doing obeisance to you or, say, stooping to observe the flora or to ease my indigestion. Generally speaking, then, to make clear both that it is a conventional ceremonial act, and which act it is, the act (for example of doing obeisance) will as a rule include some special further feature, for example raising my hat, tapping my head on the ground, sweeping my other hand to my heart, or even very likely uttering some noise or word, for example 'Salaam'. Now uttering 'Salaam' is no more describing my performance, stating that I am performing an act of obeisance, than is taking off my hat: and by the same token . . . saying 'I salute you' is no more describing my performance than is saying 'Salaam'. To do or to say these things is to make plain how the action is to be taken or understood, what action it is. And so it is with putting in the expression 'I promise that'.

(1962:70)

This distinction between explicit and whatever contrastive category is used (primitive, primary, implicit, indirect, etc.) is a complex one and has been a source of confusion in the literature. It is often suggested or implied that Austin was primarily or even solely concerned with explicit performatives, but one only has to read Austin's book to see that this is not the case (cf. Silverstein 1979; Lee 1997; Agha 2007). Austin argued, for good reason, that explicit performatives must have developed as later elaborations of primary ones – to meet the needs of explicitness and precision required by particular contexts (e.g., courtrooms, weddings, or christenings). Primary performatives obviously constitute the bulk of

---

[7] 'For example "Bull" or "Thunder" in a primitive language of one-word utterances could be a warning, information, a prediction, &c. It is also a plausible view that explicitly distinguishing the different forces that this utterance might have is a later achievement of language, and a considerable one; primitive or primary forms of utterance will preserve the "ambiguity" or "equivocation" or "vagueness" of primitive language in this respect; they will not make explicit the precise force of the utterance. This may have its uses: but sophistication and development of social forms and procedures will necessitate clarification. But note that this clarification is as much a creative act as a discovery or description! It is as much a matter of making clear distinctions as of making already existent distinctions clear' (Austin 1962:72).

what we see in ordinary interaction and are of central concern to us in this chapter. Let us reiterate that explicit vs. primary as a dimension of contrast is distinct from that of purposive action vs. effect.

We note that the matter of explicitness is more complicated than Austin imagined. A speaker's use of an explicit performative formula such as 'I $V_{performative}$ (you) (that) X' does not guarantee that the speaker is in fact doing the action so named. Consider, for instance, 'I promise you'll regret that' which is more likely to be a warning or a threat than a promise. Or consider passengers in an airport being asked (i.e., requested, and certainly not 'invited') to board the plane at another gate with 'Passengers are invited to proceed to Gate 63 to board the aircraft', and so on. Indeed Garfinkel and Sacks (1970; see also Sacks [1967] 1995) noted that if one names or describes what one is doing, this seems to be necessarily committing to doing something else, either in addition or as an alternative.

Real-Time Constitution versus Ex Post Facto (i.e., Retroactive) Formulation

A final key distinction is between the actual constitution of action in interaction (and its real-time ascription or 'recognition' by other participants) versus ex post facto or retroactive formulation or reconstruction of a piece of behaviour as having been such-and-such an action (see the passage from Austin above). Much of the literature has been concerned with speech act labels in their retroactive use to report or describe the illocutionary force of what was done, though this has not always been made explicit. Native metalinguistic vocabulary is a form of categorization, and as such it frequently involves collapsing into a single type (e.g., 'asking') actions that are conceptually distinct. The retroactive formulation of an action can be done at various degrees of distance from the target object, including in next turn (*Are you asking me or telling me?*; see Sidnell 2012b), in third position (*No, I was asking you, But I say it's really great* – see discussion in Chapter 1), and in still more distal positions as is common in various forms of reported speech (*He told me that X*).

Metalinguistic vocabulary is clearly necessary for retroactive formulation (and note that this vocabulary can include both familiar vernacular and invented technical terms), though there is no evidence that such a vocabulary necessarily has consequences for the real-time constitution of action. Yet nearly all scholarship in this area has either tacitly assumed or explicitly proposed that the real-time constitution of action is organized in relation to a set of categories more or less isomorphic with the metalinguistic vocabulary of English, and perhaps other languages (cf. Wierzbicka 1987, 2003). It is not difficult to see how this has come about given not only the powerful effects of referential projection of the kind described by Anscombe (1957, who defined intention as 'action under a description'), Silverstein (1979), and Rumsey (1990), but also the pervasive use of metalinguistic vocabulary by participants in interaction itself to retrospectively formulate action (e.g., *She was **complaining** about it, He **told** me this, She **suggested** it*).

Components and Types of Action in Interaction

We can now consider two questions that have been addressed in previous literature: (1) What are actions made up of? (2) What types of actions are there, and how many?

Distinguishing Components of an Action

The first sustained attempt to analyse action rather than merely classify it was made in Austin's *How to Do Things with Words*. Austin's goal was to understand what social action consists of. He showed that actions are simultaneously describable as 'acts' in a range of distinct but related senses:[8]

(3)
I.   Phonetic act = 'uttering certain noises'
II. Phatic act = 'uttering certain words' by means of a phonetic act
III. Rhetic act = using a phatic act 'with a sense and reference'

The three elements in (3), each of which incorporates the prior one, taken together constitute a locutionary act, as Austin put it. A locutionary act, in turn, is distinguished from further levels of description:

(4)
A.   Locutionary act = rhetic act directed at someone (3.I–III taken together)
B.   Illocutionary act = 'in what way we are using the locution'
C.   Perlocutionary act = 'produce certain consequential effects' by means of an illocutionary act

Consider an example.[9] Suppose some people take flash photographs of a painting in the art gallery. A guard approaches them and says 'You can't do that'. So they desist. Here are the different senses in which the guard's saying 'You can't do that', including their desisting as a response, can be described as 'an act' in Austin's terms:

(5)
I: She physically produced this noise: [ju: kʰaːnt du ðæt].
II: She said these words: 'you', 'can't', 'do', and 'that'.
III: She said 'You can't do that'.
A: She said to them 'You can't do that'. (= I–III together)
B: She protested against their doing it.
C: She stopped them doing it.

---

[8] The quotes in (3) are from Austin (1962:94–103); also see Clark (1996:146).
[9] The example of 'You can't do that' is borrowed from Austin (1962); we enrich it here with an imagined context.

Notice how only some of these levels of acting invoke an audience or addressee in the characterization offered by Austin. But in fact for all of them, as Clark (1996) has shown, we can be explicit about the addressee's or interpreter's role; see (6):

(6)
I: S's Phonetic act → A perceives it
II: S's Phatic act → A recognizes/identifies words and other items
III: S's Rhetic act → A understands sentence-meaning
A: S's Locutionary act → A is addressed (= I+II+III)
B: S's Illocutionary act → A understands the action in some way
C: S's Perlocutionary act → A responds to it in some relevant way

This brings out the fundamentally dialogic nature of speech acts (Clark 1996:153). Clark makes this explicit in his development of Austin's scheme, summarized here in (7):

(7) Clark's (1996) revised and relabelled scheme (after Austin 1962)
S executes production of utterances *for* A to attend
S presents words etc.   *for* A to identify
S signals/means 'sentences'   *for* A to recognize/understand
S proposes 'projects'   *for* A to consider

Could these distinctions allow us to be precise in our description and analysis of actions in interaction? Suppose someone says *Your haircut looks great*. What's the action? Is this an assessment or a compliment? The answer is that it's both. First, it is an assessment in terms of how it is composed or authored. That is, it thematizes some entity ('your hair-cut') and predicates a subjective property of it (positively valenced, in this example: 'looks great'). This merely describes the semantic properties of the utterance in terms of the form–meaning mapping of the linguistic items that were selected. It is a compliment in terms of the possible interpretants one might anticipate. That is, it makes norma-tively relevant certain kinds of responses and not others. In this case, an appropriate response might be *Thank you*. Note, of course, that another response is available, through which one would be treating it as *merely an assessment*, e.g., by responding with *Yeah, it does.*

Or, to take another example, when someone says *There's no soymilk in the fridge*, is this a statement or a complaint? Again, it's both. In terms of how it is composed or authored, it is a statement or report of a state of affairs. In terms of the set of likely interpretants, it may well turn out to be a complaint: a response might be to resist with a counter-accusation, *Well, you didn't ask me to buy any!*, and we may take this as treating the statement as a complaint. And again, one could respond to this as merely an assertion, e.g., with *Oh.*

As philosophers of action such as Anscombe point out, an action can be described in numerous ways, and at numerous levels of granularity, each of them valid for different purposes. There is no one correct description. The key is to define your frame. In the realm of social action, when we observe a person's move and wonder why that now, it is about the roots and fruits of the move: What has led to this person doing this, what is their goal, and what should I do now (subprehending as always how my reaction is likely to be interpreted)? If we observe that a person fishes for information by saying 'yer line's been busy' (Pomerantz 1980:189; see discussion above), it is not helpful to define this action as an assertion, even though it would not be inaccurate. One might want to say it is a kind of information request, though this still would not capture it, for it would not explain why the move was done in the form of an assertion, rather than simply asking, say, *Who were you talking on the phone to?* Pomerantz essentially argued that this way of fishing for information is a kind of praction (see below for this term) which she labelled a 'my-side telling'. It is a way of eliciting an ostensibly self-initiated giving of information in a circumstance where the seeker of information may not have the authority to ask straight out or may want to avoid being accountable for doing so. The label 'my-side telling' focuses on the formal properties of the behaviour (the speaker makes an assertion based on their own limited evidence, where the addressee has greater access), but a full action characterization would also require that we are explicit about what the right kind of uptake would be in the next move.

The Austin/Clark 'ladder of action' is not a taxonomy of action types. Rather it takes action and prises apart the different 'layers' that make it up. As outlined above, Austin showed that we can take the utterance *You can't do that* and separate it out into a phonetic act (She produced this noise: [ju: kʰaːnt du ðæt]), a phatic act (She said these words: *you, can't, do*, and *that*), a rhetic act (She said *You can't do that*), a locutionary act (She said to them *You can't do that*; i.e., the phonetic, phatic, and rhetic acts, taken together), an illocutionary act (She protested against their doing it), and a perlocutionary act (She stopped them doing it). The perlocutionary 'act' might also be described in another way, not in terms of what she did, but what the outcome was: i.e., the perlocutionary effect of her action was that they stopped doing it.[10]

Another way of prising apart the components of action is seen in a distinction widely made in conversation analysis between 'practices' and 'actions' (see Table 4.1) (Schegloff 1996, 1997; Sidnell 2010a). Sidnell (2010:61) defines practices as 'relatively stable features which recur across a wide range of utterance types and actions'. Actions are the social outcomes that these practices effect, in context. So, practices are tools for carrying out actions. They are devices for getting people to ascribe or 'recognize' a goal behind a piece of communicative behaviour.

While practices and actions are conceptually distinct from each other, one approach is to view them as fused. This can be referred to as a 'practions' approach (Enfield 2013:100; see Schegloff 1996, 1997; Robinson 2007), where *praction* is defined as 'a pairing of a defined

[10] See Silverstein (1979) for a meta-analysis which suggests that Austin's categories are projections from the grammar of reported speech in English, i.e., the possibilities for reporting what someone did when they spoke.

The Ontology of Action

Table 4.1 *Some practice–action mappings (drawn from Schegloff 1996; see other references there; this figure adapted from Enfield 2013:96).*

Sample practice	Example	Possible action	Possible appropriate perlocutionary effects
negative observation	*You didn't get an ice cream sandwich*	COMPLAINT	give reason; resist
positive evaluation of feature of interlocutor or just-prior conduct	*You look good in that shirt*	COMPLIMENT	say 'Thank you'; self-deprecate
tell of own limited access	*Your line's been busy*	SOLICIT ACCOUNT	provide account

practice or defined combination of practices with a defined action that these practices conventionally bring about' (Enfield 2013:100). This approach has been developed by Sacks, Schegloff, Jefferson, and their colleagues in conversation analysis – though note that much conversation analytic work is not practions-based; thus, for example, in research by Drew and colleagues, the researcher may look at a single action type or family such as 'request' or 'offer' and ask what are the different practices that can be used for carrying it out.

Unlike the other major perspectives discussed here, praction-based approaches begin with the data of recorded interaction, attempting to locate within it recurrent practices of speaking and the actions that they bring off. Beginning with such recordings encourages thinking in terms of tokens rather than types, giving direct access to the practices, which are identifiable by looking across a range of unique cases. As a result, in addition to the familiar and vernacularly labelled actions such as requesting, complaining, inviting, and so on, those working within this tradition have identified a range of previously undescribed, and indeed previously unknown, action types such as 'confirming allusions' (Schegloff 1996), 'my-side telling' (Pomerantz 1980), 'possible pre-closing' (Schegloff and Sacks 1973), among others. Many of these action types are defined in technical terms, and members of a society apparently have no conscious or explicit awareness of them (though, of course, they carry out and interpret them with ease). For example, when a speaker says 'We:ll' at a point that could be the end of talk on a topic, that speaker can be heard as doing a 'pre-closing', that is, proposing to begin the closing phase of the conversation. In addition it has been shown that the particular practices by which an action is implemented are various, contextually specific, and most important, consequential for how they are taken up (or not taken up) by recipients. For example, the action of making a complaint can be done by means of practices that merely project or imply the complaint (see Schegloff 2005), e.g., by producing a negatively valenced assessment (e.g., *This is disgusting*), by making a negative observation (e.g., *You didn't bring an ice-cream sandwich*; see Schegloff 1988), or by using an interrogative format (e.g., *Would you like that if she did it to you?*, *Am I supposed to eat this?*). While each of these can be construed as a complaint, the different linguistic practices establish different relevancies for response (see Chapter 5, below). They are, in this sense, different practions. This approach is the most attentive to the details of action simply because the details matter not only for what action a speaker is understood to be doing but also, within that, for what specific relevancies are established by doing the action in some particular way.

As Sacks noted in his first transcribed lecture (1995), the limiting case is one in which some particular goal is accomplished without the action ever having 'officially' been done. For instance, as discussed above, though institutional call takers can get callers to give their names by asking them directly: 'What is your name?', they may also do this by merely giving their own name first, thereby making relevant a reciprocal identification by the caller with the same format.

The Ontology of Action

Taxonomizing Actions

In the last section we looked at some approaches that ask what are the components of a single action. We now turn to approaches that seek to identify the different types of distinct actions. Is there a list of possible actions? Are there infinite possibilities? Is the possibility space organized hierarchically? Let's consider two theory-motivated proposals for a general division of actions into types.

One possible branching of action types is Tomasello's (2008) three macro 'social motivations': requesting (to secure another's help for your own goals), helping (to give your help for another's goals), sharing (to further mutual goals). These three macro action categories are grounded in a theory of human sociality that posits a line of development, in both phylogeny and ontogeny, from simpler and less prosocial actions under the rubric of requesting, up to the more demanding and more longitudinal relationship-oriented actions that come under the rubric of sharing, including phatic communion, narratives, and other uses of language whose practical effects are less immediate. A virtue of Tomasello's three-way model is that it defines the inherently social-relational phenomenon of action in social-relational terms.

By contrast, Searle defines actions in terms of types of intentional state that an individual may have. He writes that 'there are 5, and only 5 types' of speech act (Searle 2010:16). Searle (1979, 2010) proposes a taxonomy of actions that is grounded in the set of basic human intentional states: beliefs, desires, intentions, and feelings. Searle (2010:69 and *passim*) proposes an 'exact analogy' between four basic speech acts and four basic intentional states or possible relations of mind to world:

assertives ≡ **beliefs** (judged on whether they fit the way the world is)
directives ≡ **desires** (judged on whether the world comes to fit to them)

commissives ≅ **intentions** (judged on whether the world comes to fit to them)

expressives ≅ **feelings**

Thus, Searle (1983) begins with a basic theory of intentional states, grounded in individual cognition, and derives from it a higher-level set of social/communicative actions. (In addition, Searle has a fifth type of speech act – the declarative – that is not based on a basic psychological state unless perhaps imagining; see Searle 2010.) It is a conceptual framework, and Searle does not attempt to account for any aspect of reality with it. Indeed, in a late response to Rosaldo's (1982) anthropological critique of his arguments (especially Searle 1969, 1976, 1979), he writes (2006:26–7):

When I published a taxonomy of the five basic types of speech acts (Searle 1979), one anthropologist (Rosaldo 1982) objected that in the tribe (*sic*) that she studied, they did not make very many promises, and, anyway, how did I think I could get away with making such a general claim on the basis of such limited data? But the answer, of course, is that I was not offering a general empirical hypothesis but a conceptual analysis. These are the possible types of speech acts given to us by the nature of human language. The fact that some tribe does not have the institution of promising is no more relevant than the fact that there are no tigers at the South Pole is relevant to a taxonomy of animal types. I am discussing the logical structure of language and getting the categorization of possible types of speech acts.

A second version of a taxonomy of speech acts begins with the lexical semantics of speech act verbs. In one sense this would seem to be closer to the work that Austin began, but later elaborators have not developed the underlying conceptual account the way Austin would have presumably wanted (or the way Searle did). This account begins with the observation that all languages include a vocabulary of speech act verbs and that these have certain affordances, principal among them being that they can be used in conversation to describe what a speaker did in saying something. Moreover, speech act verbs appear to be organized – within a language – into 'families', such as requesting, pleading, commanding, ordering, directing, instructing, and so on (Wierzbicka 1987, 2003). There is a sense in which these words denote variant actions within a single functional class.

The vernacular label issue is a complex matter of categorization. If we analysed vernacular labels for speech acts in the same way we analysed vernacular terms for natural kinds or cultural artefacts, we would say that they reflected the speakers' worldview. But in addition, action labels have unique affordances for action itself and play a role in the regimentation or accountability of action, in ways that other types of categorizing words do not. The use of speech act categories, being meta-semiotic as they are, should have an impact on how people behave.

The approach of categorizing actions by reference to vernacular labels suffers from a problem that plagued Austin, namely that it inevitably raises but seems unable to answer the basic question of the relationship between (type-level) descriptions of action and action itself. In fact, most of it (e.g., in conversation analysis) either overlooks or denies the fact that vernacular speech act terms carry conceptual baggage from the historical culture from which they are derived (cf. Wierzbicka 1987, 2003, 2010, on English). We need, then, to distinguish between ideology (as enshrined in vocabulary; i.e. the set of actions 'we' think we have and think 'we' do) and practice (as observed in utterances; i.e., the actions we actually do and are treated as having done by our recipients). There are, of course, occasions in which actions indeed get named in the course of doing them (e.g., saying *You're not supposed to agree with him*, which explicitly describes a token utterance as a speech act of 'agreeing'; see Schegloff 1992). Participants in interaction sometimes say, in so many words, what they were doing in speaking the way they do, and in so saying they may be justifying, explaining, or holding others to account for, what was done. That the resources for doing this vary from language to language is entailed by the fact that the meanings of words vary from language to language.

An Alternative Account: A Generative View of Action

The two questions discussed in the last section – What are the components of an action? And what types of action, if any, are there? – relate directly to the hearer's problem of figuring out what a speaker is trying to do by saying something. Our focus here is on the problem that faces any addressee of an utterance: what is the speaker of this utterance doing, or trying to do? How should I react?

We argue that a hearer does not need to (consciously or otherwise) classify an action as being of a certain type in order to know how to deal with it. A hearer uses the components of a move to figure out on the fly an appropriate token response to that particular token move. It may happen that certain token actions share features with many others and so are readily interpreted by means of heuristics that have been successfully applied before (Schelling 1960; Gigerenzer, Hertwig, and Pachur 2011, among others). But actions can be dealt with at the token level and need not be seen as tokens *of action types* at all. We want to say that the taxonomy of action types is fundamentally meta-semiotic in nature. It is primarily an analyst's construct.[11] A radical version of our claim would be that there are no actions, only the parts of actions. To be able to analyse interaction using action category labels might be a descriptive convenience, but it is not a veridical claim.

Our account therefore contrasts with those which suggest that for participants to ascribe an action to another person's talk, they must take a particular bit of conduct (e.g., the utterance *That's a really nice jacket*) and assign it to some particular action type or category – e.g.,

[11] Remembering that ordinary people, i.e., participants in interaction, can also act as 'analysts', e.g., in cases of third position repair where prior talk is analysed as having constituted some particular action.

'compliment'. This is a *binning* approach, in which the central problem is taken to involve recipients of talk (or other participants) sorting the stream of interactional conduct into the appropriate categories or bins. The mental operation might be translated as 'that's a compliment' (Levinson 2012) or in subtler versions 'that's a possible compliment' (Schegloff 2005). These accounts appear to involve a presumption about the psychological reality of action types that is akin to the psychological reality of phonemes (Sapir 1933; see also Dresher 1995). That is, for the binning account to be correct, there must be an inventory of actions just as there is a set of phonemes in a language.[12] Each token bit of conduct would be put into an appropriate pre-existing action-type category. The binning approach thus also suggests that it would be reasonable to ask how many actions there are. But we think that to ask how many actions there are is more like asking how many *sentences* there are. Here lies the key to our account: Actions are generated out of constituent elements of context and code that we already need in order to infer utterance meanings and appropriate responses. There is no need to add another level, conscious or otherwise, at which action categorization would be done.

In the following sections we present two cases to illustrate the way interpreters can figure out how to respond appropriately to others' behaviour, based exclusively on components available in the talk and bodily conduct, and without us having to categorize the move to which they respond 'as action X' or equivalent.

A Non-Linguistic Example: Action Construal and Object Transfer

Consider the difference between two commonly used action type-labels: 'request' and 'offer'. One way of conceptualizing the difference is to distinguish in terms of who is the beneficiary: if it is a request, the one who instigates the action is the beneficiary; if it is an offer, the

---

[12] The analogy should not be overextended: Obviously, inventories of phonemes differ greatly from language to language.

beneficiary is the addressee. But a problem with this is that often, we cannot know – nor, it appears, can the participants – whether one is actually a beneficiary relative to the other. Indeed, it can be argued that the answer to the question 'who benefits?' is always a matter of construal anyway. What matters, instead, is *the publicly claimed construal of the behaviour*. Thus, we sometimes have no doubt what the action is: *Would you mind passing me that plate?* is readily labelled as a request, while *Shall I take that plate for you?* is readily labelled as an offer. The transparency of the action in each case is a product of the fact that the publicly construed (claimed) beneficiary is made explicit in the coding of the utterance ('passing *me*', 'for *you*', etc.). In other cases it is hard or impossible to tell whether the action should be labelled one or the other. But in just these cases – crucially for the point we want to make here – it remains clear how one ought to react, i.e., hand the plate to the other person.

Consider an example (Rossi 2014).[13] At the end of a meal, Mary is clearing the plates and holds her hand out across the table towards John, whose plate is in front of him. John responds by picking up his plate and putting it in her hand. What was the action that Mary did by holding out her hand? Was it a request from Mary for John to pass the plate? Or was it an offer by Mary to take the plate from John? Our point is that whether it was a request or an offer is not an issue for the participants. John's appropriate response did not require him to distinguish between these two possibilities. By handing the plate to her, he resolved the interpretation of what she was doing to a level that was *adequate for the situation*. No further resolution in action ascription was necessary.

We argue that John is able to respond in an appropriate way purely on the basis of the components of Mary's behaviour, rather than by recognizing a general action category that Mary's behaviour instantiated.

[13] Thanks to Giovanni Rossi: we have benefitted from discussion with him of examples such as these in his project on recruitments in Italian interaction (Rossi 2014, 2015; Rossi and Zinken 2016).

To see how this works, we begin by noting that in the example we are considering, Mary and John face a simple, and general – surely universal – problem: that of transferring objects between people. Locally speaking, transfer of an object – the plate – is a goal. In order to achieve that goal, the people involved have available to them various means. In this particular case, Mary has employed a set of signs she can assume John will readily recognize, and she has exploited the common ground that she knows that they share. Here are some of those signs:

- She is looking at John while holding out her hand and is thereby 'addressing' him.
- Her hand shape indexes holding the plate.
- Her body is oriented in a certain way.
- Her arm has a certain trajectory.
- Her behaviour has a relation to prior conduct, continuation of an ongoing, recognizable activity of clearing the table.
- Mary is host, John is guest.

The most relevant interpretation of this ensemble of signs in context is that John should now pick up his plate and put it in her hand. Other interpretations are thinkable (e.g., that she is doing a bodily depiction of some behaviour that happened on another occasion) but are less likely. For the participants to decide whether this was an 'offer' or a 'request' may go beyond the requirements of the moment. For us the analysts to decide would involve us making claims for which no evidence is available – for example, who was the beneficiary of the object transfer. That's a matter of construal, and no claim to such a construal has been made here.

Now, if Mary had said *Would you mind passing me that plate?*, then we would happily say it was a request or, better yet, that she had formulated it as a request which is to say that she was, by the format of the utterance, construed as the beneficiary of the projected action. And she would be accountable for having done so. But this does not mean the addressee had to, or did, categorize it as a request. (Though note, of course, that another key measure of how it was taken could be found in a linguistic component of the response, if there was one – e.g., saying *Sure* versus *Thanks* as he passes the plate.) The proper or desired response can be calculated in the same way as we have described for the earlier, seemingly ambiguous, situation. The addition of explicit linguistic wording may not be in the service of making 'the action' recognizable at a specific level but may have more to do with the potential accountability of the move being made. Had Mary said *Shall I take that plate for you?*, she would be making explicit her construal of the situation in action terms; i.e., that she's doing it *for John*. This would lead us to label it – if we had to label it – as an offer. The linguistic component may, though need not, make explicit some of the defining components of action recognition, bringing us back to the on-record nature of the claim of who's benefitting (and the associated accountability).

A Linguistic Example: 'Pre-Closing', 'Assertion', 'Complaint', or 'Request'?

We now move into the linguistic domain and look at an example in which a listener is faced with the task of inferring how they are to respond on the basis of elements of a complex linguistic construction, in combination with the sequential placement of the speaker's move. Our example gives further support to the idea that a binning approach cannot account for much of the data of ordinary talk-in-interaction. Such an approach will not adequately predict how participants in fact respond. We sketch an alternative account in which participants attend to a range of components of a move – both turn-constructional and sequential features – in order to assess what a prior speaker is doing in a given utterance, and in turn, how they are to react. In our example, sisters Lottie and Emma are talking on the telephone:

(8) NB:1:6:4, 4:15
```
01  Lottie:   °Oh I ↓love tuh gee I ride mine all[th' ti:me.°
02  Emma:                                       [°Ye:ah.°
03  Lottie:   I love it.
04  Emma:     hhh WELL honey (.) Ah:ll (.)
05            pob'ly SEE yih one a'these da:y[s,
06  Lottie:                                  [Oh: Go:d
07            yeah[(ah wish)]=
08  Emma:         [ ehh huh ]=
09  Lottie:   =But I c- I jis'[couldn' git do:wn ( )
10  Emma:                     [Oh-u ↓Oh I ↓know=
11            =I'm not as[kin' yih tih c'm dow- ]
12  Lottie:              [J e e : z i z   I   mean ]I jis
13            (0.2)
14            I didn' have five minutes yesterday.
15  Emma:     Ah don' know how yih do i:t.
16            (0.3)
17  Lottie:   Ah don' kno:w. nh huh
18  Emma:     You wuh: work all day tihda:y.
19            (0.3)
20  Lottie:   Ye:ah.
21            (0.2)
22            Jis git well I'm (.) by myself I'm kin'a cleanin
23            up fr'm yesterday.
```

To this point the conversation has covered a range of topics and in line 01 Lottie is talking about riding her bicycle. Then at lines 04–05 Emma produces the turn 'hhh WELL honey (.) Ah:ll (.) pob'ly SEE yih one a'these da:ys'.

This utterance has several properties of interest to us here:

- It comes at the analysable end of talk on a topic (riding bicycles).
- It is prefaced with 'well'.
- It does not raise a possible next topic of discussion.
- It looks forward to some future occasion when the sisters will see one another (albeit in an unusual way).

All of these features of the turn mark it as what Schegloff and Sacks (1973) described as a possible 'pre-closing', a first move to initiate a closing sequence. Two common types of response to such possible pre-closings are (1) to produce a matching turn that similarly passes on the opportunity to raise a next topic and thereby forwards the closing sequence, and (2) to raise a next topic of conversation and thereby defer the move towards the closing sequence. Lottie does neither of these things.

We can see that Lottie responds in a way that suggests she has heard in Emma's turn a *complaint* about her. Specifically, she responds by excusing herself, explaining that she 'just couldn't get down', and that she 'didn't have five minutes yesterday'. This occasions Emma saying, 'I'm not asking you to come down' at line 11.

A binning approach would have to analyse this in terms of ambiguity. Thus, Emma's talk at lines 04–05 *could* have been heard as a pre-closing, a complaint, or even a request (Emma later explicitly denies this). Lottie simply picks one possibility and responds to that: here, she takes it as a complaint. But there is no need to say that the talk is one action or the other, in terms of these labels. We think it is none of these. What we see instead is that in the details of its design, Emma's turn makes available to Lottie a set of resources for building an understanding of what she is doing. Lottie's evidence for an understanding is drawn from Emma's specific choices of words, grammatical construction, prosody, positioning of the utterance in relation to what has come before, and so on.

Returning to Lottie's response to Emma, then, we can notice that she understands this to be something new, not apparently related to the talk about bicycles and riding. Second, she seems to respond primarily to two parts of the talk in line 05 – 'probably' and 'one of these days'. This is a recurrent position in conversation where participants routinely make plans to get together at some specific time in the future. In this context, Emma indicates uncertainty by selecting 'probably' and 'one of these days' in designing her turn. Both expressions – one expressing doubt that they will in fact see one another, the other making reference to a time that is insufficiently precise to allow for planning – suggest a departure from the norm, thus implying a problem. It has already been established (in earlier talk) that Emma had hoped to see Lottie, and so, in this context, the talk suggests that Lottie is responsible for their not getting together. We see, then, how multiple elements of the high-lighted move's formulation serve as bases for an interpreter's construction of understanding, where this understanding then provides grounds for producing a response that effectively categorizes (though, importantly, does not describe or otherwise *type*-categorize) the first move in a certain way.

Consider this example now in light of the three fundamental conceptual distinctions we made earlier in this chapter. The first distinction was between purposive action versus given-off effects of one's behaviour. Lottie's problem at lines 06–07 is how to respond to what Emma has said. As we have noted, various features of placement and design converge to suggest that 'hhh WELL honey (.) Ah:ll (.) pob'ly SEE yih one a'these da:ys' is meant to initiate pre-closing, that being Emma's possible purpose or intention in producing the utterance. But there are obvious complications here. For one thing, we can describe Emma's purposive action at different degrees of granularity. While apparently designed to accomplish possible pre-closing, Emma's utterance is simultaneously an assertion. It asserts about a likely future state of affairs. This is available to Lottie as a possible hearing of the utterance and thus as a possible target for response. Consider, then, what Lottie says: 'Oh: Go:d yeah'. In form, at least, this constitutes *agreement* with the proposition Emma has asserted. Moreover, this provides the basis from which Lottie launches her excuse. And of course the excuse, as we have already noted, treats Emma's turn not as a possible pre-closing, not as an assertion but rather as a complaint.

This suggests, then, that a given utterance makes available various understandings of a speaker's purpose or intent and that a response, or next utterance generally, targets one or more of these, thereby treating that *as the purposive action* that that utterance was doing (see Goffman 1976). A wide variety of compositional and positional resources may bear on what an utterance is understood to be doing. These are the elements of a generative account of action. It is important to note that the components of a given utterance need not necessarily point towards a single obvious action interpretation. Rather, the various features may point in different directions resulting in unclarity as to the most appropriate response (for studies that deal with aspects of this see, for instance, Sidnell 2010b; Sidnell 2012b; Heritage 2012).

As we have argued above, it is possible and, from a methodological point of view, crucial to distinguish such purposive action from the multitude of effects that any given utterance may have. Consider, again, Emma's utterance 'hhh WELL honey (.) Ah:ll (.) pob'ly SEE yih one a'these da:ys'. There are ways in which the design of the utterance in question indexes the relationship between the participants. Perhaps most obviously, by addressing Lottie as 'honey', Emma claims that they are related to one another in such a way that her calling Lottie 'honey' is appropriate (see Enfield 2013: Chapters 5 and 10). Moreover, the phonetic production of the talk here suggests a casualness and lack of formality that is appropriate to social intimates. A more complex issue here has to do with the indexical effects of the purposive action that the speaker is understood to be engaged in (whether it be complaining, asserting, or proposing closure). To do an action presupposes that the participants stand in such a relation to one another that that action is appropriate, e.g., one tells or reports something to an addressee who is uninformed, one advises an addressee who is less expert, less knowledgeable, or less experienced, one commands an addressee who is subordinate, etc. (see Rosaldo 1982 on this point). And another set of indexical effects relates to the assertive character of the utterance – that is, Emma conveys by the use of 'pob'ly', a degree of uncertainty with respect to the truth-value of the proposition asserted. And of course there are effects of a more mundane sort: in speaking here, Emma displays involvement in the ongoing activity, sustains the conversational turn-taking system in operation, suggests an understanding of the point at which this conversation has arrived, and so on.

The second distinction we made earlier in this chapter contrasted explicit versus primary performatives. Explicit performatives, in which the action apparently being performed is named by a speech act verb in the first-person, non-past denotational structure of the utterance itself, are rare in conversation. One view might be that the action is distinct enough, and it's just that there is no available word for the action being done in 'hhh WELL honey (.) Ah:ll (.) pob'ly SEE yih one a'these da:ys'.[14] Schegloff and Sacks (1973) noted that the closing of a conversation can be initiated in one of two ways. Specifically, either the reason (what they describe as the 'warrant') for closing can be announced (e.g., *well that's all I wanted to say* or *I should go, the kettle's boiling*) or it can be embodied by reciprocal turns-at-talk that pass on the opportunity to raise further topics of conversation, thereby conveying – giving off rather than giving – that the participants have nothing left to say. These are not explicit and primary versions of the same action. Rather, they are different actions. A possible pre-closing such as saying *We:ll* at the key moment may result in the same outcome as saying *I have to go*, but it is not the same. A possible pre-closing is inexplicit about what is being done. This inexplicitness is part of what defines it as a possible pre-closing. It is not equivalent to saying *I propose we initiate the close of this conversation* (something we can safely say almost never happens) despite the fact that it is, in a certain sense, just that: a proposal to initiate closing.

---

[14] This was the case for all sorts of actions before they were described by analysts (e.g., 'confirming allusions', 'my-side tellings', etc.); although a 'my-side telling' could easily be vernacularly glossed as 'asking', but not, of course, during the course of the turn itself.

And finally, there is our third distinction: the contrast between the real-time constitution of action and the ex post facto (i.e., retroactive) formulation of action. It is obvious that actions can be named (e.g., *She praised me*), described (e.g., *She talked down to me*), indexed (e.g., *Why did you do that?*), and so on. The implications of this are, however, not well understood. In our example we can note that after Lottie responds to Emma's utterance with an excuse or explanation, Emma remarks, '↓Oh I ↓know= =I'm not askin' yih tih c'm dow-'. Here, then, Emma treats what Lottie has said as already known to her and thereby as constituting a recipient-design error.[15] She goes on to characterize what she was doing in negative terms, as '*not asking* you to come down' (see Schegloff 1992:1306).

In the following example from a news interview panel, the formulation is positive, with the interviewer (Intwr) noticing that he has violated the ground rules of the activity by 'telling' rather than 'asking' (see Sidnell 2012b for further explication):

(9) The_Sunday_Edition_RESERVES_6_11_05
```
01 Intwe:    has got to be: lo:cal, regional, and pro[vincial.
02 Intwr:                                            [.hhhhhh
03           Indian people on reserves. (.) don't own the
04           land they live on.
05           (0.4)
06 Intwe:    That's:: [(
07 Intwr:             [it's held by the crown.
08 Intwe:    wuh-uh- well: uhm:
09 Intwr:    It's owned by the crown [an' administered
10 Intwe:                            [yes.
11 Intwr:    by [thu::h
12 Intwe:       [yes.
13 Intwr: →  Here I am telling you what it (h)[i(hh)-
```

[15] The 'oh' obviously does not convey that Emma has been informed by what Lottie has said – that would be inconsistent with what she goes on to say - 'I know'. Rather the 'oh' seems akin to the 'oh-prefaced responses to inquiry' or 'oh-prefaced responses to assessments' that mark what the prior has said as inapposite and requiring a shift of attention (see Heritage 1998, 2002).

In both cases just discussed, the formulation of a prior action is done in third position (Schegloff 2007), but other positions are, of course, possible. So, for instance, there are cases in which an interviewee asks, in second position, 'are you telling me or asking?' (see Heritage 2012). And of course, extra-local formulations are common, for instance, in reports of what happened in another interaction and so on.

Thus, although the vast majority of action is produced and recognized without any such ex post facto, retroactive formulation, this is nevertheless an ever-present possibility and thus must figure in a comprehensive account of action in interaction. Action ascription is accomplished, in the main, without recourse to formulation and associated taxonomies. In interaction, the question of 'what a speaker is doing' does not require definitive or fine-grained resolution. Rather the matter is addressed, on the fly, with understandings that are tacit, provisional, and never needing to be more than sufficient to allow for the production of appropriate and effective response.

Discussion

We have argued for a generative account of action ascription which focuses on the token inferences a recipient makes based on multiple components of an utterance, and where this inferred understanding is displayed in the token response that they produce. This account is superior, we argue, to one that is based on assumptions about the category or type of action – assuming some sort of action inventory – that an utterance is designed by a speaker or understood by a recipient to accomplish.

We want to be clear about what this does and does not entail. First, we are not denying that speakers engage in purposive action; indeed this is central to our account. Rather, we are suggesting that such purposive action is not usefully understood in terms of categories or types which constitute an inventory. Instead, purposive action emerges through a token-level inferential system. Action 'types' are available only through forms of retroactive (and sometimes proactive) formulation but are not required for orderly production and recognition of action in interaction. Second, we are suggesting that a crucial feature of action in interaction has to do with the accountability structures to which participants hold one another. In a basic sense, to paraphrase Cavell, 'we must mean what we say'. A speaker will be understood to be meaning – and therefore to be doing – just what his or her words conventionally imply. A speaker cannot simply choose not to mean what he or she has said. Similarly, in producing an utterance with certain components, the speaker unavoidably does something and what he or she is understood to do, and is held accountable for, will certainly bear some relationship to those components. Thus, in our example, Emma's use of 'probably' and 'one of these days' triggered a particular inference for Lottie, as we saw from Lottie's response. As Austin was well aware and as later commentators elaborated, more explicit performatives are designed so as to be maximally clear about what is being done and to specify more precisely that for which the speaker is accountable (see 'I promise to be there' vs. 'I'll be there').

If action is conceived in terms of pre-existing categories or types, then the job of the recipient would be to identify the appropriate bin into which a particular turn should be put into. But with a generative approach we can begin to describe, for any particular case, the specific linguistic practices used as bases for inferences about purposive action. We have focused on a complex case – the seemingly ambiguous 'Well I'll probably see you one of these days' – and the reader might object that our account does not apply to most actions most of the time. The reader might object that all sorts of actions like 'requests', 'offers', 'invitations', 'complaints', etc. are usually directly recognizable, straightforward, and clear and thus that a binning analysis is fine. But this does not follow. Our account is more parsimonious because one can still get to the straightforward response by working directly from the parts. And in any case, the truth is that not many moves are straightforward in interaction. Anyone who has tried the exercise of working through a conversational transcript line by line and labelling each line with an action category knows that it is a hopeless task.

Indeed, our approach predicts that it would be hopeless to *label the action*, while it will be straightforward to know *what an appropriate next move would be*. As we have stressed, these two things are not the same. Interactants are far from hopeless in knowing how to respond. Our point is that they can know how to respond quite reliably by working up from turn components and finding a token solution, and not by having to assign the whole turn to an action category.

Now, finally, think about this from an actor's point of view. In order to select the right elements in formulating a move, a speaker must anticipate the effect that those elements will have on the interpretive behaviour of a listener. The interpreter's task is what drives the speaker's formulation (Enfield 2009, 2013). The speaker's job is to design a turn on the basis of a set of available components: phonetic, lexical, syntactic, and other resources. Speakers select components such as words, intonation patterns, and grammatical constructions, but – crucially – they don't select actions.

We conclude, therefore, that participants in interaction do not need to recognize action types or categories in order to respond appropriately (or inappropriately for that matter). This is the central claim that we have tried to make in this chapter. Other theories that have addressed the problem of action ascription seem to assume that such ascription involves assigning each bit of conduct to an action-type category, essentially a process of labelling. Our view is that when we are analysing such moves in the flow of interaction, we are not labelling actions but, rather, considering the details of particular turns-at-talk for their relevance in deciding what to do next and how to do it. And all of their details are potentially relevant to what people are understood to be doing. Action category labels are convenient heuristics, but they are, ultimately, neither necessary nor sufficient. Category labels cannot substitute for practice-based analysis of situated social action.

Part III

Action and Human Diversity

Part II

FIVE

Collateral Effects

Does speaking one language rather than another have consequences for how we think and act? Anthropologists, linguists, philosophers, and psychologists have all sought to answer this question. The enormous literature spanning back at least 200 years encompasses everything from formal logic and analytic philosophy, to naturalistic observation and psychological experiment, to work bordering on literature and fiction. Everyone from Edward Sapir to George Orwell, from Franz Boas to Toni Morrison has had a say on how the language one speaks does or does not affect one's understanding of, and place within, the world that surrounds them.

Linguistic Relativity

The question of linguistic relativity has been central to the anthropology of language (Gumperz and Levinson 1996; Lucy 1997; Everett 2013), though the methods for answering the question, and the kinds of answers given, have undergone significant transformation (Leavitt 2011; Enfield 2015). Within the existing anthropological literature, we can discern at least two distinct versions of a relativity argument. The first – associated with the founders of linguistic anthropology – links language-specific patterns of grammar to thought (in the general sense of mental representations

of states of affairs and the inferences that arise from these representations) and habitual behaviour (Boas 1911; Sapir 1921, [1927]
1949, [1931] 1964; Whorf [1939] 1956a, [1940] 1956b, [1945] 1956c).
This version has received significant attention from linguists and
psychologists and, over the last twenty-five years or so, has been
pursued in a wide range of psychologically informed studies that
use experimental methods to test the cognitive consequences of
language diversity (Lucy 1992a, 1992b, 1997; Pederson et al. 1998;
Boroditsky 2001; Gentner and Goldin-Meadow 2003; Winawer et al.
2007; Majid, Boster, and Bowerman 2008, *inter alia*). Studies in this
vein have become increasingly sophisticated in terms of method
and in terms of their grounding in linguistic typology. At the same
time their perceived relevance to social and cultural anthropology
has lessened because of the increasing focus on referential functions of language rather than the numerous other functions, and on
individual psychology rather than culture or distributed linguistic
practice.

A second version of the relativity argument was hinted at by Hymes
(1966), made explicit by Silverstein (1976, 1979), and subsequently
elaborated by a number of linguistic anthropologists (see, e.g.,
Errington 1985, 1988; Briggs 1986; Ochs 1988, 1990, 1992, 1996; Hanks
1990; Rumsey 1990; Agha 1994, 2007). In contrast to the earlier
emphasis on referential and predicational aspects of language,
Silverstein focused on the *indexical* relations between speech and
its context of occurrence. Indexicality is a sign-function in which
a signified is linked to a signifier by a relationship of contiguity
(classic examples include smoke being taken to signify fire, a knock
being taken to indicate someone at the door, and so on; see Peirce
1955; Parmentier 1994a, 1994b; Kockelman 2005). The basic argument
is that by the very act of speaking, speakers both indexically presuppose and create, moment-by-moment, a *context*. Thus, in saying
Do you know the way to Conn Hall?, the speaker indexically

establishes (among other things) an addressee (a 'you').[1] Now consider the difference between English and French. In French, a speaker must choose between address with *tu* or *vous* (and of course if you say *tu* you can be heard as not saying *vous* and vice versa), whereas in English there is only one second-person pronoun (Brown and Gilman 1960). These different forms convey something about the relationship between speaker and addressee and about the context in which the talk takes place. Within some specific set of contextual presuppositions, every act of address in French thus takes aspects of the relationship between speaker and hearer and makes them explicit, yet these same aspects need not be articulated in English at all.[2] This difference between the two languages appears to have consequences for the contexts that their speakers establish through speaking one or the other of the languages. It is a simple example because the range of alternatives (*tu* vs. *vous*) is so narrow.

Things become considerably more complex when we consider person reference and address in Vietnamese where the range of alternatives is extensive, and where a number of perspective-taking strategies are also used. And the argument may also be applied to other domains, not just the social deixis of *tu–vous* type alternations or Vietnamese person-referring forms. Even more basic, perhaps, are the indexical signs (primary among them deictics such as *here* and *now*) by which participants convey and thus constitute or construe the here and now of any actual social encounter. If the first version of the relativity argument emphasizes the consequences of language diversity for the world *perceived*, the second focuses on the world *indexed* (and thus produced)

---

[1] Let us clarify what this means. When I ask you a question, and because I ask it, you become an addressee. Obviously my question has not created *you*, but rather it has created a *status* (in the sense of a set of entitlements and responsibilities) that you now fill (e.g., you are now accountable for not answering the question).

[2] Explicitness is important because it relates to whether speakers potentially 'go on record' and may thus make them accountable for what they have said or done. This can be seen in relation to T-V address forms in Jacquemet (1994).

in different ways through different languages, in and through the very act of speaking.

To these now well-established versions of the relativity argument, we add a third. The first version began with language conceptualized as a system for thought, and the second with speaking as 'meaningful social behavior' (Silverstein 1976). The third version begins with practices of social interaction and the particular forms of social action which they provide for.[3]

Our thesis is that different grammatical and lexical patterns of different languages can provide different opportunities for social action. Since Wittgenstein (1953) and Austin (1962), it has been recognized that by speaking we are not simply, solely, or primarily engaged in describing the world, depicting it, or indexing it in some way. Rather, by speaking we are acting in it. When you say *That's a really nice jacket*, you've not only described someone's clothing but also given them a compliment (see Pomerantz 1978). When you say *The traffic was terrible today*, you've not only described your commute, you've complained about it. And when you say *Could you give me a lift?*, you've not only asked a question, you've made a request.

When we examine conversation, we see that participants themselves can use subsequent turns-at-talk as evidence for whether, and how, they have just been understood by the other. This participants' method can also be exploited by researchers as a methodological and analytical lever. Thus, to determine the particular action which some

---

[3] Silverstein (1987) makes this same distinction between indexicality and purposive action. Our 'third locus' relates to Silverstein's 'function₁', which concerns 'the purposive, goal-oriented use of speech (or equivalents) by intentional individuals in specific situations of discourse, each such usage constituting a "speech act" or "speech event"' (p. 23). His 'function₂', in contrast, 'consists of multiple relationships of existential implication among isolable elements/aspects of a communicative situation. In particular, we can see linguistic elements as the principal system of indexicals, the elucidation of which is a third kind of functional explanation' (p. 31). This is the domain of the 'second locus' of linguistic relativity, discussed above.

bit of talk achieves, we can look to see how it was taken up (or not) in subsequent talk (see Sacks, Schegloff, and Jefferson 1974:728–9 on the so-called 'next-turn proof procedure'). This is crucial because it solves one of the more difficult methodological problems of all relativity arguments (see Lucy 1992a, 1992b): how to show that a grammatical or lexical peculiarity has non-linguistic (that is cognitive, cultural, action-relevant) consequences. The first version of the relativity argument has come to rely on forms of experiment using measures such as memory and inference to demonstrate such consequences. The second version typically relies on native-speaker testimony and ethnographic description. A feature of the third version is that the consequences, while clearly non-linguistic, are nevertheless internal to the data.

We will illustrate this third approach to linguistic relativity by investigating the different ways in which a specific purposive social action is carried out using as a 'vehicle' the lexico-grammatical resources of three different languages: Caribbean English Creole (Sidnell 2009b), Finnish (Sorjonen 1996; Hakulinen and Sorjonen 2009; Sorjonen and Hakulinen 2009), and Lao (Enfield 2007a). The idea is to use the controlled comparison of a single social action (what we call 'epistemically authoritative second-position assessment', defined below as the action of agreeing with what someone has just said while simultaneously signalling that one has greater authority to have said it; cf. Heritage and Raymond 2005).[4] Each case study reveals the specific grammatical resources employed in that language as well as the associated interactional consequences.

---

[4] To be clear: if there is a basic action here, it is 'agreement'. The 'epistemically authoritative' part of what we describe here is laminated onto agreement. So it would, of course, be quite impossible to *merely* claim epistemic authority without embedding this in some action (e.g., agreement). It is perhaps reasonable to describe, as Heritage and Raymond (2005) do, epistemic authority as being 'indexed' here. This would suggest that our case study, while focusing on action, also introduces some features of the second version of relativity we discuss.

Collateral Effects Defined

A lexico-grammatical structure will be an appropriate tool or vehicle for carrying out a certain social action so long as its semiotic affordances make it well-suited to effecting that action – e.g., to the extent that people will readily ascribe to it the function it is being used for. But because any such lexico-grammatical structure will have other structural properties as well (including other meanings), other semiotic affordances are unavoidably introduced. The structure is selected because it has a certain functional feature, but other properties of that structure will be ushered in, and these in turn will be features for other functions, or else these collaterally selected properties may turn out to be bugs, bringing unwanted results. Either way, the selection of a linguistic structure based on one feature will inevitably introduce other features that give rise to what we shall refer to as collateral effects, that is, side effects of the selection of a specific means for some ends (see below).

Our three example cases are useful for a number of reasons. First, a good deal is known about the phenomenon central to these cases: 'responses to assessments' (see especially Pomerantz 1984; Goodwin and Goodwin 1987; Heritage and Raymond 2005). Second, the languages differ significantly from each other in structure. Both the Lao and the Caribbean English Creoles are highly analytic languages largely devoid of any inflectional morphology. Finnish, by way of contrast, has an extensive set of inflectional morphemes (suffixes) that attach to both nouns and verbs: nouns are inflected for case (nominative, accusative, partitive, genitive, locative etc.); verbs are inflected according to the person and number of the subject; other verbal suffixes convey distinctions of tense, aspect, mood, and so on. While Caribbean English Creoles use word order to convey grammatical relations or semantic roles such as agent and patient, in Finnish, word order is relatively free and these relations are expressed by inflections on nominal arguments.

Lao is like the Caribbean Creole in being highly analytic but differs – crucially for our purposes – in that it has an elaborate system of final particles.

Social Interaction: The Progressive Realization of Understanding in Action

Our third locus for linguistic relativity is social interaction, not just in a general sense that would encompass much of what we have been discussing so far, but in the specific sense of the sequences of interlocking actions that people carry out by using language in social settings (Schegloff 1968, 1996, 2006, 2007; Heritage 1984; Goodwin and Heritage 1990; Goodwin 2002, 2006; Drew 2004). Social action is about doing things, where this 'doing' involves other people. Language is the central tool. We use it to get other people to do things for us, to help others or inform them of things, to share experience with them, to affiliate with them, or indeed to disaffiliate (Enfield and Levinson 2006; Tomasello 2008; Sidnell 2010a). The perspective that is required for studying this domain of human activity is an *enchronic* one (Enfield 2013), i.e., a focus on the move-by-move, normative frame of 'interactional time', as a complement to other, more familiar temporal-causal perspectives in anthropology and related disciplines (microgenetic, ontogenetic, phylogenetic, dia-chronic, synchronic, etc.; see Enfield 2014a).

Research on language in interaction using the methods of con-versation analysis has shown that it is both possible and necessary to examine language use at the micro level in order to understand just how these forms of social action are accomplished, and how intersubjectivity is achieved. In the social sciences, intersubjectiv-ity – joint or shared understanding between people – is typically explained in terms of convergent knowledge of the world. On this view, the world exhibits objective characteristics, and to the extent that different actors apply equivalent and valid procedures for generating knowledge of the world, they will effectively converge in their knowledge and understanding of their circumstances (Heritage 1984:26). A related solution to the problem of intersubjectivity invokes the notion of a common culture as the resource through which 'the individual's grasp of reality is mediated' (Schegloff 1992:1296).

As we have outlined in previous chapters, conversation analysts have developed a rather different account of intersubjectivity. One of their key insights (Sacks 1995; Sacks et al. 1974) was that ordinary people exploit the systematic properties of conversation in reasoning about it 'on line'. For instance, participants in a conversation can inspect next turns-at-talk as evidence for if and how their own talk has been understood. Displayed misunderstandings can then prompt the initiation of repair in 'third position' as in the following example. Here, 'the press relations officer in a Civil Defense headquarters is asking the chief engineer for information to be distributed to the media' (Schegloff 1992:1303).

(1) Third position repair – from Schegloff (1992)
```
01   Annie:     Which one:s are closed, an' which ones are open.
02   Zebrach:   Most of 'em. This, this, [this, this ((pointing))
03   Annie:                              [I 'on't mean on the
04              shelters, I mean on the roads.
05   Zebrach:   Oh!
06              (0.8)
07   Zebrach:   Closed, those're the ones you wanna know about,
08   Annie:     Mm[hm
09   Zebrach:     [Broadway...
```

In line 01, Annie asks a question. In the turn at line 02, Zebrach not only attempts to answer it but, by virtue of producing a response, displays an understanding of Annie's line 01 inquiry. From this response, Annie is able to surmise that there has been a misunderstanding of her talk in line

01. It appears from the evidence in line 02 that Zebrach has made a wrong interpretation of 'which ones'. Annie is able to repair the problem in lines 03–04, and the course of action under way is then re-engaged on the basis of the new understanding which Annie's correction provides for. As Schegloff (1991:158) notes: 'The ordinary sequential organization of conversation thus provides for displays of mutual understanding and problems therein, one running basis for the cultivation and grounding of intersubjectivity.'

Consider the following case from the opening of a telephone call between two friends, focusing on lines 04 and 05:

```
(2) Deb and Dick
            (ring)
            (r[
01   Deb:    [Hello:?hh
02   Dick:   Good morning.=
03   Deb:    =Hi:, howareya.
04   Dick:   Not too ba:d. Howareyou?
05   Deb:    I'm fi::ne
06   Dick:   Howdit g[o?
07   Deb:            [.h Oh: just grea:t,<everybody:st-still here.
08   Dick:   Oh really(h)=
09   Deb:    =Yeah
10   Dick:   Oh they stayed. Okay.
11   Deb:    Yea:h
```

Dick asks 'How are you?' and Deb responds with 'I'm fine'. This simple exchange seems almost vacuous, but in fact it tells us a lot. Deb's response in line 05 to Dick's 'How are you?' in line 04 displays a range of basic understandings of that turn (Schegloff 1992): By starting to talk at this moment (and not earlier), Deb shows an understanding that Dick's turn was possibly finished (see Sacks et al. 1974). By producing an answer, Deb shows that she understands the previous turn to be a question. By answering with a description of her personal state, Deb shows that she understands the turn to be a wh-question (involving a question word like *who, where, how,* etc.) rather than a yes–no interrogative. By responding with *fine* rather than *terrible* or *fantastic,* Deb shows an understanding of what this question is doing in this environment (a routine opening enquiry, not to be taken literally, etc.). On this view, the use of language and other forms of communicative behaviour in social interaction centrally involves the production and recognition of *purposive action* (as defined in Chapter 4). So when Deb says 'I'm fine' in response to Dick's 'How are you?', she shows that she understood Dick's turn to be one of those personal state inquiries that does not call for a completely 'honest' response but rather an indication of whether she has any particular bad or good news to tell Dick (see Sacks 1975; Jefferson 1980; Schegloff 1986).

We see, then, that the turn-by-turn organization of talk provides for a continuously updated context of intersubjective understanding, accomplished *en passant* in the course of other activities. These publicly displayed understandings are provisional and contingent and thus susceptible to being found wanting, problematic, partial, or simply incorrect. Where a first speaker finds the understanding displayed by a second speaker's turn inadequate, they have recourse to a mechanism for correcting it (an organized set of practices of repair; see Schegloff, Jefferson, and Sacks 1977; Schegloff 1992; Hayashi, Raymond, and Sidnell 2013).

Relativity of Action in the Balance of Agreement and Authority

In these examples a participant used the available resources of the English language (potentially along with other forms of behaviour such as hand gesture) to compose a turn that a recipient was able to recognize as accomplishing some particular action. Does the fact that the words were spoken in English and not in another language have any bearing on how that action is accomplished? Given the well-documented facts of significant if not radical language diversity in the world, we should expect the answer to be yes. We should expect that language diversity has consequences for the constitution of action through talk-in-interaction.

One view might be that the structural characteristics of a language are inconsequential in this regard: The same actions get done, in the same ways, regardless of the language used. Another might be that the available repertoires of social actions are entirely incommensurate across languages (cf. Zinken and Ogierman 2013; Zinken 2016). Between these extremes lies the position that we want to defend: some social actions are more readily carried out, or are carried out in specific ways, by speakers of a given language by virtue of the lexico-grammatical properties specific to that language. Moreover, while 'the same' action in a functionally general sense (e.g., request, complaint, agreement) may be possible in different languages, in reality these actions will differ in specifiable and significant ways across the languages. Because an action must be done in a different way, it may have rather different implications for subsequent action within the same sequence.

This idea suggests a new programme of research. Our goal here is to explore the direction such a programme might take. If we begin with an illustrative functionally defined target action that we might expect speakers of any language to want to carry out in social interaction, we can then compare the specific lexico-syntactic resources that languages make available as tools or 'vehicles' for carrying out this action. Do the differences between these linguistic vehicles for action correspond to differences in the specific nature of that action in the case of each language?

We explore this question by focusing on an action that we will refer to technically as an *epistemically authoritative second-position assessment*. By 'assessment', we mean the use of an evaluative expression (such as *She's a swell gal*) to express a person's stance towards someone or something, often in the grammatical form of an assertion. (Note that in the below examples we also widen the scope beyond 'assessments' to assertions more generally.) Such stance-taking is an important device for building, maintaining, and adjusting the affiliative links that structure our social networks. When someone makes such an evaluation in 'first position' in a conversation – i.e., without being prompted to do so by another speaker's prior assessment – this is often followed in conversation by a similar assessment by a second speaker (thus, in second position) as a way for the second speaker to align (or not) with the first in stance.[5]

So, a second-position assessment is a person's statement of subjective evaluation that immediately follows, and thus appears to be occasioned by, and agreeing with, another person's evaluation of the same thing. This is a common pattern in conversation, and one might assume that it is unlikely to be particularly fraught. But as recent research on English has shown (Drew 1991; Heritage and Raymond 2005; Stivers 2005; cf. Stivers, Mondada, Steensig 2011 for similar work on other languages as well), even while people are fully agreeing on the sentiment being expressed (e.g., *That child is a handful*), they are careful to monitor and explicitly acknowledge who has primary rights or greater authority to make such an evaluation. In an illustrative case from Heritage and Raymond (2005; also Raymond and Heritage 2006), two elderly women talking on the phone each voice the opinion that James, the grandchild of one of the women, is a mischievous boy, but they tussle – in subtle

---

[5] One property of this second position assessment is that it may appear to be prompted by the assessment just prior, implying that the second speaker might not have thought to make this evaluation on her own. The reasons for this cannot be detailed here and indeed are only recently being explored (see, e.g., Enfield 2013: Chapter 10). What we can say is that there is a pervasive preference for agreement in conversation (Sacks 1987). As such, when someone agrees with a prior assessment they are often vulnerable to being heard as just going along with what the other said. This structurally introduced bias partially explains the use and availability of pragmatically marked agreement forms such as *of course* in English (see Stivers 2011).

ways – over who has the primary epistemic authority to make this evaluation. The notion of relative epistemic authority is captured by Heritage and Raymond with a simple notation 'K-plus' (notation = K+) for the state of 'knowing better than the other', as opposed to 'K-minus'. In their example, the woman who is the grandmother of the boy James has the primary epistemic authority to make this assessment.[6]

As Heritage and Raymond show, a sequence of first assessment followed by second assessment is harmonic when the second speaker is also the one who has less authority to know ('K-minus'). Correspondingly, they show that when the sequence is *dis*harmonic – i.e., when the speaker who produces the agreeing evaluation in second position is the one who knows, or should know, *better* – then speakers will go out of their way to redress a first assessment's implied claim to epistemic priority.[7] They do so through practices of speaking: a less knowing speaker may manage the disharmony by downgrading their evaluation if it is in first position (e.g., with *I think*, etc.), while a *more* knowing speaker may *up*grade their evaluation if it is in *second* position (e.g., through the use of dedicated preface forms such as *oh*; see Heritage and Raymond 2005).[8]

Our interest here is in the specific format of marked practices of speaking that manage the disharmony of a second-position assessment

[6] A complication is that one's 'official status' may be invoked as a basis for authority, even where this does not align with the reality (e.g., a nanny who spends more time with a boy than his mother does may know the boy better, but may defer to the mother on certain claims anyway; cf. Enfield 2013: Chapter 10 for discussion).

[7] 'Better' in this context can have to do with rights to know, degree of access, how recently the information was acquired, and so on.

[8] Heritage and Raymond (2005) discuss four practices in English for accomplishing K+ second assessments. Two of these upgrade by suggesting that the position was already held or settled. The other two practices involve usurping the 'firstness' of a previous assessment. Although the authors describe these multiple practices for accomplishing K+ second assessments, they do not discuss their functional differentiation in terms of either distribution or what we have described as collateral effects. Because languages differ significantly at all levels of structure, the range of choices in one language cannot be exactly the same as in any other. Moreover, where we have found alternate practices in a given language (for instance, 'I know' vs. 'if' prefaces in Caribbean Creole, or VS vs. SV word orders in Finnish), they are functionally distinct, providing speakers of these languages with markedly different systems of resources for action.

being made by a speaker with higher authority to make the assessment. We will refer to this balancing act – agreeing with what someone just said, while signalling that one has greater authority to have said it – as a 'K+ second assessment', or 'K+2A' for short. Think of it as a two-part task: (1) you want to agree with what was just asserted by the other person, but (2) you want to signal that you are in a better or more rightful position than that other person to assert it. As we shall see, the grammatical resources for this practice are different across languages, and these differences affect the nature of the action such that it cannot be done in exactly the same way across the languages. Because each language's strategy draws on lexico-grammatical resources that are used for other functions as well, this introduces *collateral effects* on how the action is done, as we explore below.

Collateral Effects Again

Before we present the cases, let us further clarify what we mean by collateral effects. The notion of collateral effects is of central importance to our argument, and we believe that it has special promise for new research in the relation between language, cognition, and action.

Here is how a collateral effect arises. First, one has a certain end or goal; one wants to do something. Second, in order to achieve that end or goal, one must select a means. Third, the means that one selects will necessarily have a certain structure; not only will some elements of those means be directly responsible for bringing about the desired ends, but these elements will co-occur, often in relations of dependency, with other features of the structure as well. Finally, these co-occurring other structural features will introduce effects that weren't necessarily selected for. These are collateral effects: side effects of something that was selected as means to a required end.

Take a simple example. Suppose you are a student photojournalist and your instructor gives you the task to 'meet with a real person and succinctly capture their personality'. You are given a choice to submit your work in the form of either a written paragraph of prose or an untitled photograph. Both of these is a means to solve the task, but their different affordances introduce different collateral effects. A collateral effect of using a photograph is that it would be difficult to avoid revealing the person's physical features, and thereby things like their age, gender, state of health. By contrast, the affordances of prose would readily allow the writer to leave those aspects of the person unrevealed.

As an example from the realm of symbolic systems, consider expressive differences between the modalities of spoken language versus the hand gestures that accompany speech. Imagine that your expressive goal is to describe a motion event, say, 'He left the room'. If your selected means are in spoken language only, in the same way that you can describe someone in prose without revealing their physical features, you can verbally describe this scene without making any information available as to the direction or speed of the event being described (as in English *He left the room*). But if one chooses to depict this event using hand gestures, one is necessarily showing the motion as having happened at a certain speed and in a certain direction (regardless of whether one wanted to show this, or whether an onlooker interprets that speed and direction to be part of what you intend to say). Of course, we often select co-speech gesture precisely so that we can exploit these affordances of the modality. But consider sign language of the Deaf, in which one will most heavily rely on the manual means for linguistic expression, and not as an alternative to the vocal channel. When the manual-spatial modality is used as a means to expressive ends, these means not only express spatial relations such as motion, but – differently from the vocal modality – other information about that motion is necessarily expressed as well. These collateral effects are a product, or by-product, of the selection of means to ends.

K-Plus Second Assessments: A Three-Language Comparison

We now turn to our comparison of these kinds of effects in the pragmatic realm of social action.

Caribbean English Creole: If-*Prefaced Repeats*

Our first example comes from the Caribbean English Creole spoken on the island of Bequia, St Vincent (from research by Sidnell, e.g., 2009b). The action of K+ second assessment is routinely done in this language by prefacing a repeat of a prior speaker's talk with 'if'. First, let us describe the more common function of this practice of *if*-prefacing in the language.

In most varieties of English, one standard way of forming polar questions (i.e., yes–no questions) is to invert the ordering of subject and auxiliary verb in simple declarative constructions (Quirk et al. 1985); *You're going for a nap* becomes *Are you going for a nap?* Such inverted syntax can be preserved in repeats which initiate repair so that, for instance, repair is initiated with forms such as *Am I GOing?* or *Am I going for a what?* In the creoles of the Caribbean there is no subject–auxiliary inversion in polar questions. Indeed, there is no syntactic category of auxiliary verb for such an inversion to operate upon (see Winford 1993). Instead in these varieties a turn's status as a question is constituted through a range of features of design and context. None of these features (intonation and prosody, directed gaze) can be transferred (unproblematically) to a turn that other-initiates repair in order to show that the turn being targeted was understood to be a polar question (see Sidnell 2009c for further discussion). This is where *if*-prefacing comes in.

In their basic canonical use, then, *if*-prefaced repeats are used to initiate repair of a prior turn that is formatted as a polar question. Pat's turn at line 03 of Example (3) is an instance. Here Pat and

Benson are sitting side by side in the yard that adjoins Benson's small house. It is a week after Carnival and Pat has stopped by for a visit with Benson's neighbour.

(3) #187_Q2 qt 51:50

01   Benson: yu biin hii fu kanival (.) Pat?
                    were you here for Carnival Pat?

02   (.)

03   Pat: →   if mi bin wa?
                    if I was what?

04   Benson: Bekwe fu kanival?
                    Bequia Carnival?

05   Pat: yeah:
                    yeah

When Benson asks Pat in line 01 if she was in Bequia for Carnival, Pat responds by initiating repair with *if mi bin wa?* 'If I was what?' – an *if*-prefaced repeat. The preframing *mi bin* 'I was' combined with the question word *wa* 'what' isolates *hii fu kanival* 'here for Carnival' as the trouble source to be repaired. By prefacing the turn with *if*, Pat also shows that she heard the turn addressed to her as a polar question. At line 04, when Benson repairs the reference, he preserves the status of his turn as a question by producing it with rising intonation. At line 05 Pat answers the question with a 'yeah'. The function of the *if*-preface in line 03, then, is to show that the one initiating repair heard that the turn containing the trouble source was produced as a polar question. Thus, in their basic, canonical use *if*-prefaced repeats initiate repair of a prior question turn and in so doing begin an insertion sequence that breaks the contiguity of the first and second parts of an adjacency pair (Schegloff 2007).

If-prefaced repeats are also deployed in a quite different sequential context – specifically, in response to assessments. In this environment, *if*-prefaced repeats are second assessments that agree with a prior assessment. Example (4) provides an illustration. Here Shanka and Kiki are sitting in their family yard with three young children close by. At line 01, Kiki directs one of these children – Zaria (who is Shanka's cousin and Kiki's niece) – to move and, in close succession, to 'take that thing', an object on the ground in front of her. Kiki completes the turn with a question about the whereabouts of Zaria's cousin Roxanne. Zaria responds only to the final part of the turn, apparently pointing to where Roxanne is. Kiki then directs her attention to the slightly older girl Naksin. As Kiki produces this turn, Zaria runs away. This occasions Shanka's evaluative assessment of Zaria at line 06 – *Wailnes Zaria a kom wid* 'Wildness Zaria comes with'. At line 07 Kiki responds with *if Zaria wail?* 'if Zaria is wild'.

(4) #134_Q1 qt 25:38

01   Kiki: Zaria muv from de.=tek a ting.
                 Zaria move from there. Take that thing.

02   wapa Rakzan.
                 Where is Roxanne.

03   (3.0) ((Zaria pointing to where Roxanne is))

04   Kiki: Naksin lii shii:. tek da- an ting- Jak ting.
                 Naksin leave her, take that and thing, Jack's thing

05   (2.0) ((Zaria runs away))

06   Shanka: W̲ailnes Zaria a kom wid.
                 Wildness Zaria comes with

07   Kiki: if Zaria wail?
                 if Zaria is wild

08   (0.4)

09   Naksin kom.
            Naksin come here

We can see, then, that this assessment sequence is occasioned by
a complex set of visible behaviours and witnessable actions – the failure
to comply with the directives, the flailing hand gestures, the running away.
Notice that unlike the case shown as example (3), here the *if*-prefaced
repeat does not elicit any response from the recipients. Indeed it seems to
close the assessment sequence, as the talk turns to other matters.

Consider next example (5). This begins with Donna calling to her
nephew (who is off camera). Although he appears to respond, he does
not comply with the request to 'come here'. After Kiki beckons the same
boy again, Benson turns to Donna and remarks 'he's rude you know'.
This initiates a string of assessments culminating in an *if*-prefaced
repeat.

(5) #139_Q1 qt 39:25

01 Donna: Gusnel kom bai hee
                 Gushnell come over here.

02 (Gushnell):   (for yu)

03 Kiki: (Gusnel) kom he.
                 come here.

04 Benson: °hii ruud yuno°
                 he's rude you know
                 ((Benson turns behind him to look at Donna))

05 Donna: ai noo hi ruud
                 I know he's rude

06   (1.2)

07	Benson:	riil ruud.
		real rude
		((returns gaze in front of him))

| 08 | | (0.4) |

| 09 | Ezekiel: | huu ruud. |
| | | *Who's rude?* |

| 10 | Benson: | da boi [de. |
| | | *That boy there.* |

| 11 | Donna: | [if hi ruud? |
| | | *if he's rude?* |

The *if*-prefaced turn in line 11 once again closes this extended sequence of assessments. With it, Donna seems to have the last word and the talk turns to other concerns. Note that in both this and the previous example the original first-position assessment is a vehicle for complaining about a non-participant, third-party.

As pointed out above, in their basic interactional environment, *if*-prefaced partial repeats initiate repair on a polar question. In other words, *if*-prefaced partial repeats convey that their speaker has heard a previous turn containing the trouble-source to be a polar question. In these last two examples (4 and 5), the practice is used to treat a prior assessment as if it were a polar question. It is important to recognize in this respect that in examples (4) and (5) the turn to which the *if*-prefaced assessment responds is not in fact a question. Moreover, in (4) and (5) the *if*-prefaced turn does not initiate a repair/insertion sequence as it does in (3). Rather, with these *if*-prefaced second assessments, second assessors are doing agreement.

One piece of evidence for this is that, like other agreements (and preferred actions more generally), these turns are closing-implicative, meaning that they help to bring topics or sequences to a close (though see our discussion of VS-formatted responses in Finnish, below). By contrast, dispreferred actions and disagreements in particular tend to be sequence-elaborative and engender more talk on the same topic. So notice that in example (4), after the assessment sequence at lines 06–07, the talk turns to other matters (Kiki beckons Naksin). And in example (5) a long string of assessments concludes with an *if*-prefaced repeat at which point the participants again turn to other matters.

But these *if*-prefaced turns go beyond just agreeing. By responding to the first assessment as if it were a polar question, the *if*-prefaced turn treats a first assessment as a question and thus as epistemically downgraded relative to a declaratively formatted assertion (see Heritage and Raymond 2012 on the notion of an 'epistemic gradient'). By considering the context in which the practice is used, we find evidence in support of this analysis. In (4), for instance, the first assessment is produced by Shanka, who is Zaria's cousin, and the second by Zaria's aunt (Kiki), who is partially responsible for her. The assessment here is a complaint and thus the *if*-prefaced format of the second assessment may be selected to deal with a situation in which Kiki feels she needs to reassert her greater rights to evaluate the child (see Raymond and Heritage 2006). And in (5), evidence of the participants' orientation to the matter of differential epistemic rights is found both in the prior talk and in the social relations by which they are connected to one another and to the person being assessed. Here Benson is assessing Donna's nephew. The design of the initial exchange is sensitive to Donna's greater epistemic rights. Specifically, Benson produces his first assessment as a question (line 04, °*hii ruud yuno*° 'he's rude you know'), in this way inviting Donna to confirm it, which she does in a particularly explicit way (line 05 *ai noo hi ruud* 'I know he's rude') not only confirming but explicitly referring to her claimed knowledge state.[9]

---

[9] This is an alternative format for accomplishing a K+ second assessment in this variety – one which would appear to engender quite different collateral effects (e.g., it is not closing implicative).

The sequence continues with Ezekiel initiating repair (*huu ruud* 'who is rude?'). After Benson repairs the reference with a demonstrative referring expression, Donna responds to the initial assessment again, now with an *if*-prefaced turn. Here again, then, relative rights to assess are at issue: this is, after all, Donna's nephew that Benson and Ezekiel (a family friend) are assessing. The participants' orientation to the matter of differential rights to assess, here grounded in different social relations to the person, is made explicit through the design of the initial assessments. In using the *if*-prefaced second assessment at line 11, Donna is pushing these already recognized rights to their limit – claiming, in effect, the last word on the matter of whether the child is rude.

If-prefaced second assessments work the way they do because they treat a prior assessment as if it were a question. *If*-prefacing takes its sense and import in this environment from its canonical use in the other-initiation of repair of a prior polar question. Its use in K+ second assessments is arguably derivative of a more basic use in initiating repair, and this in turn appears to be a reflex of grammar in languages that do not use syntactic inversion to form polar questions. The example of *if*-prefacing thus shows how specific grammatical patterns can have consequences for action in talk-in-interaction, as a result of the features of a lexico-grammatical vehicle for action that are imported as collateral effects in doing that action. Specifically, in initiating repair of polar questions (and in reporting them, see Sidnell 2009c) second speakers may preface the turn by *if*. Once established as an 'interrogative marker', this item, *if*, may be adapted to other contexts, thus opening up language-specific possibilities of social action.

As we have seen, with an *if*-prefaced second assessment, a second speaker not only agrees with a first assessment but also claims greater epistemic rights to assess the matter. And a further collateral effect has to do with how this practice shapes the context for subsequent talk. Specifically, *if*-prefaced second assessments are closing implicative to such an extent that their speakers can be heard as having the last word (or trying to have it – see Sidnell 2009c for a case in which the attempt fails). So in this case we see at least three interactional functions fused in a single practice: (1) agree with prior assessment, (2) claim epistemic priority relative to the first-assessment speaker, (3) move to close topic. As we shall now see, while there are similar practices in other languages, these are not identical.

Finnish: Word Order Variation

Our second example of the consequences of language specific-grammatical patterns for social actions comes from research on Finnish by Hakulinen and Sorjonen (2009; Sorjonen and Hakulinen 2009). These authors discuss a range of alternative second-assessment formats, all of which are used to agree with a first assessment.

Two typological features of Finnish turn out to be relevant in the formulation of utterance formats as means of agreement to assessments. First, Finnish is a language that has, from a grammatical point of view, 'free word order' (cf. Vilkuna 1989). This means that, for example, verb initiality can be deployed for a number of discourse purposes, one of them being the responding to questions, assessments and negative assertions. Secondly, in Finnish, a fully grammatical clause can be formed without an overt subject: with an anaphoric zero, a response is tied to the utterance of the prior speaker.

(Hakulinen and Sorjonen 2009:149)

The result is that Finnish speakers have five distinct ways of repeating some portion of a first assessment in order to agree with it.[10] For the purposes of illustrating our argument, we will focus on

---

[10] The authors describe these responses as forming a paradigm, labelling them as follows (where V = verb, S = subject): V, V+V, V+S, S+V, V+particle. And of course there are additional ways of agreeing that do not involve repetition.

just two of these responses – those which Sorjonen and Hakulinen describe as 'VS' and 'SV' respectively. These alternatives are shown in the example below (adapted from Sorjonen and Hakulinen 2009):

(6) Sorjonen and Hakulinen 2009

1st assessment:

Se	mekko	on	hieno
That	*dress*	*is*	*great*

Response:

se on "SV"
it is

on se "VS"
is it

According to Sorjonen and Hakulinen, the first of these responses conveys the independence of the second speaker's stance – that the second speaker, while agreeing with the proposition, held the view being expressed independently of it being articulated by the first-assessment speaker.[11] The second response conveys that the second-assessment speaker agrees with the first but views the matter from a different perspective. That difference may or may not be explicated in the ensuing talk.

The following example illustrates the second, VS format. Here the participants are talking on the phone and discussing the weather. In the preceding talk, each has described the beautiful weather in their present location (L is at home and A is at her cottage in a place where L also has a cottage). Where the transcript begins, A transitions from talk about the weather conditions of the day to 'autumn' generally:

---

[11] As the authors note, this is similar to the use of 'oh' in English in second assessments (see Heritage 2002).

(7) Sorjonen and Hakulinen 2009

```
09  A:        Nyt   kelpais        ollak[i. Mut kyllä sie]l  on
              now   worth.would be.CLI but  sure  there is
              Now it would be something. But it is really

10  L:                                  [Ai( )              ]

11  A:        ihanaa heti          kun   ei    sada.
              lovely immediately   when  NEG   rain
              lovely there as soon as it's not raining.

12  L:        ↑Nii, [Joo,
              Right, Yeah,

13  A: →            [.hh Kyl se on: syksy    on niin
                     PRT it is:  autumn is  so
              .hh It really is: the autumn is so

14     →      mahdottoman kaunis.[h
              impossibly  beautiful
              extremely beautiful.h

15  L: →                         [On  se.=
                                 is   it.

16  A: →      =.Jo[o
              Yea

17  L:        [>Kyllä mä vi-  ei    viikonloppuna menen
              sure I    we-  NEG   weekend       go.1
              I'm surely wee- at the weekend I'm going

18            <.hhh mä meen kans t- kääntää ↑maat ja.hh
                    I  go.1 also  turn    lands and
              .hhh I'm also going to dig the land over and.hh
```

19 laittamaan kuntoon varmuuden
   put   shape.ɪʟʟ safety's
   put everything in shape to be

20 vuoks kaikki jos (.) j<u>o</u>s sitte ei tuu
   sake everything if if then Ø ɴᴇɢ comes
   on the safe side if (.) if one doesn't get to

21 enää   °mennyks°
   anymore going
   go there °anymore°.

So, as the authors explain, while the participants here clearly agree on the beauty of autumn, they are nevertheless positioned rather differently with respect to the proposition 'the autumn is beautiful'. A is at this moment enjoying the beauty of the Finnish hinterlands in autumn, and by expressing this as a bald, timeless statement of fact (the autumn is so extremely beautiful) can perhaps be heard as anticipating future occasions on which these same conditions will be enjoyed. L, on the other hand, is, it turns out, preparing to sell her cottage. After she agrees with the assessment 'the autumn is so extremely beautiful' using a VS-formatted response, she goes on to explain that she plans to visit her cottage, potentially for the last time, the next weekend to 'put everything in shape'. This, as Sorjonen and Hakulinen note, is the beginning of a troubles telling and thus conveys quite explicitly the difference in perspective which the VS-formatted second assessment adumbrated. Key to our argument here is the authors' observation about this and other examples like it: namely, because the VS format implies a difference of perspective, it can be topically elaborative. That is to say, use of this format can establish the relevance of an unpacking of the different perspective of the second speaker and thus result in elaboration of the topic.

  Consider now the following instance in which the response is SV formatted:

(8) Field note, spring 2007

01   A: Se on ihan hirveen hyvä opettaja.
             it is quite terribly good teacher
             He is just an extremely good teacher.

02   B: →   Se on.
             it is
             He is

The authors explain:

By responding with the format *se on* B both asserts agreement with A, and
implies the independence of her stance. In the prior talk, B was the one who
was telling the others about the specific event, portraying the success of the
colleague's teaching. Now that A presents her assessment, B's turn can be
heard as agreeing but simultaneously confirming A's stance.

(Sorjonen and Hakulinen 2009:288)

The following provides a more complex case but one for which we have
a fuller sense of the context, including the ensuing talk which provides
the evidential basis for our claims about the character of the action being
performed.

(9) (Kotus, T1208: 61, Eastern Finland, hairdresser's)

01   C: Joo.
             Yeah.

02   (33.7) ((H. cutting client's hair))

03   H: →   .mt Voi mahoto   mite o itsepäine hius.
             oh impossible how is obstinate hair
             .tch Oh my god what obstinate hair.

04   C: Mm-m.

05   (0.6)

06   C: →   .nf   Ne   on.
                they   is.

07   (2.0)

08   H: Mite sie sitä   aina   kotona   ite   laitat.
            how you it-PAR always home.ESS yourself make.
            How do you set it at home by yourself.

09   C: No geelillähän sitä   pittää °mh°,
            well gel.ADE.CLI it-PAR Ø must
            Well you have to use gel °mh°,

10   (0.7)

11   muottoilla.
            Shape
            to shape it.

Here the first assessment in line 03, 'mite o itsepäine hius', has a singular referent and employs a lexical referring expression rather than a pro-term. The response in line 06 substitutes a plural pro-term for *hius* 'hair' but is nevertheless formatted as SV. Notice now that the independence of C's stance – that she felt this way prior to the current occasion, independently of what has just been said – is presumed by the ensuing question from H ('How do you set it at home by yourself?'). This very question presumes that the client has encountered on previous occasions the obstinacy that the stylist has remarked upon and the client confirmed.

So in the Finnish case, there are at least two distinct formats for agreeing with a prior assessment while at the same time asserting independent epistemic access [K+] from second position. The availability of word order alternations (among a number of other grammatical features; see Hakulinen and Sorjonen 2009) makes possible a distinction between [K+] = independent access and [K+] = different perspective. And this has the collateral consequence that the use of the VS format can be topically elaborative rather than closing implicative (in contrast to the Creole case we have just seen; cf. also Lao, below).

In both the Creole and the Finnish cases, the second, agreeing, K+ assessment involves repeating a portion of the prior talk. But the languages differ substantially in the way the repeated portion is elaborated by the available lexico-grammatical resources of the language. In the Creole, speakers use a form the basic semantics of which derive from its use in other-initiation of repair (i.e., *if-*) to cast the prior assessment as a question, thereby retrospectively transforming the other speaker's first assessment by suggesting it was said with uncertainty. In Finnish, relatively free word order makes possible an alternation between VS- and SV-formatted repeats. This provides for a distinction within the broader category of K+ responses such that the VS format implies a different perspective.

By comparing the cases of Creole and Finnish, we see that they both provide speakers with a way to do K+ second assessments, but the linguistic resources that are picked up and used as tools for this specific action are associated in the two languages with other, non-equivalent functions. This non-equivalence gives rise to different collateral effects on the specific nature of the action in the two languages. We now turn to our third case, Lao.

Lao: Perfective Particle Lèq1

Lao is a Southwestern Tai language spoken in Laos, Thailand, and Cambodia (Enfield 2007a). An important grammatical feature of this language, like many other languages of the mainland Southeast Asia area (Enfield 2005, 2017), is the frequent (though not obligatory) use of final particles. Lao has a large inventory of illocutionary particles that typically occur in final position relative to a turn-constructional unit (i.e., turn-finally, either attached to a clause or free-standing noun phrase; Enfield 2007a: Chapter 4). These are words that occur at the ends of utterances (whether those utterances are full 'sentences' or fragments), with the function of indicating certain grammatical meanings such as temporal features of an event (tense, aspect), or shades of meaning concerning the attitudes and expectations of the speaker, often in relation to the addressee.

There are three broad functionally defined categories of Lao final particles: interrogative, imperative, and factive. Loosely speaking, the factive particles are appended to assertions, forming a set of contrasting semantic specifications concerning the epistemic status of a proposition given aspects of the speech event. For example, one may take a simple proposition such as *man2 phèèng2* 'It's expensive' and add different particles for different effects: with the particle *dêj2*, a speaker makes a claim that the assertion is news to the addressee (*man2 phèèng2 dêj2* 'It's expensive you know'); with the particle *sam4*, a speaker makes a claim that the proposition is unexpected or surprising given the context (*man2 phèèng2 sam4* 'But as it turns out, it's expensive'); or with the particle *lèq1*, a speaker makes a claim that that the assertion is already or independently known to be the case (*man2 phèèng2 lèq1* 'It is indeed expensive').

One way in which speakers of Lao manage the action of making a K+ second assessment is to append the particle *lèq1* to the repeated evaluation or assertion. This particle, exemplified in the previous paragraph, is termed a 'factive perfective'. It is elsewhere used to signify completion of an action or event, a meaning arising from its association with a perfective verbal marker *lèèw4* (which is also a full verb meaning 'to finish'; Enfield 2007a:180ff.). The connection between the two meanings 'completedness of an event' and 'prior establishment of the truth of an assertion' should be obvious: generally, if someone can assert that a narrated event is completed, they convey that in the speech event they have independent knowledge of its truth. Syntactically speaking, as a final particle, *lèq1* may occur appended to clauses or noun phrases (usually demonstratives), as in the following two examples, respectively.

(10) Lao

01 A: bòø qùt2 lèq1
        NEG lacking FAC.PRF
        Indeed (it's) not lacking.

(11) Lao

01 A: nan4 lèq1
        DEM.NONPROX FAC.PRF
        (It's) that (very) one.

The communicative function of *lèq1* is to signal independent, prior, or markedly precise knowledge of the assertion. In example 12 (from a video recording of an informal visit between in-laws in rural Vientiane, Laos), Speaker M uses *lèq1* to signal this sense of special precision. The sequence begins in line 02 with Speaker K's question as to whether Speaker P has fully recuperated yet after an accident. Speaker P responds with a minimal confirmation (in line 03), and Speaker M (P's wife) follows this up with an elaboration, first stating that P has now been able to walk for two days, and then clarifying with the more precise statement that it has in fact been three days. This clarification (in line 06) is marked with *lèq1*.

(12) 020727a:195

02 K: khaj1 dèè1 laaj3 teep5 laø mbòø=
        improve somewhat much very PRF PCL
        (Your condition has) improved quite a lot, right?

03 P: =mm5=
        Yeah.

04 M: =haa3-kòø ñaang1 daj4 sòòng3 mùù4
        just   walk   can   two   day
        (He is) just able to walk, (since) two days (ago).

05   (1.0)

06   saam3 mùù4 niø lèq1
        three day   this FAC.PRF
        Three days today (in fact)

Similarly, in the next case (example (13) from a video recording of two neighbours talking in a rural Vientiane village), Speaker S is talking to Speaker K who has just arrived in the village by car. Just prior to the segment supplied here, Speaker S has been asking about another man named Loy (K's son), and S has asked whether or not Loy had also just come with K to the village. In the first lines of the example (lines 15–16), K explains that when Loy had the chance to get in the car to travel to the village, he had not done so. In line 18, S asks if this is because Loy was tied up with work. When K replies that he wasn't and that Loy had simply not wanted to come, this information is marked with the final particle *lèq1* (line 20). It conveys an air of finality to what is being said, in line with the perfective semantics of *lèq1*. Accordingly, the appended question in line 24 cannot be heard as anything other than rhetorical, and indeed the sequence closes here completely, with 20s of silence ensuing.

(13) 030806a:160

15 K: phòø-dii3 vaa1 khùn5 lot1 juu1 han5
       right.when say   ascend vehicle LOC there
       Right when (we) said (let's) get in the car there

16   bak2-looj3 phen1   bòø maa2 baat5-niø
       M.BARE-L. 3SG.POL NEG come PCL
       Loy, he didn't come, now

17   (0.8)

18   S: khaa2 viak4
           stuck   work
           (He was) tied up with work (you mean?).

19   (0.7)

20   K: kaø   bòø khaa2 lèq1
           TLNK NEG stuck FAC.PRF
           (He was) not tied up!

21   (0.2)

22   tang4 bòø maa2 sù-sùù1 niø lèq1
           intend NEG come that's.all TPC FAC.PRF
           (He) just didn't come, that's all!

23   (1.5)

24   K: siø   khaa2 ñang3
           IRR stuck   what
           What would ((he)) be tied up with?

25   (20s)

As these examples show, a central function of *lèq1* is to convey a sense of 'finished', a function that is clearly traceable to the source of this word in the verb *lèèw4*, meaning 'to finish'. When this meaning is imported from the realm of the narrated event (i.e., what the utterance is about) into the realm of the speech event (i.e., the speech act participants, and their relationship), it comes to mean 'there's nothing more to be said here now'. It is this component of the final particle *lèq1* that makes it appropriate as a vehicle for managing the K+ second assessments that we have focused on above. We now turn to examples in which *lèq1* is used for carrying out this type of action, i.e., where *lèq1* is appended to second-position assessments (or assertions, to be more accurate with reference to the Lao examples below) where the speaker is agreeing on the one hand, but pushing back against an apparent claim to authority embodied in a first-position assessment, on the other.

In the following example (14), two elderly villagers, Mr Ka and Mr P, are having an informal conversation at the village home of Mr P. They are both lifelong residents of the rice-farming plains and nearby forests and waters around the area of Vientiane. The occasion is a visit by Ka (and his wife) to P (and his wife). The two men don't know each other well, and as they discuss the local forests and the various herbal medicines that can be found there, a sense of competitiveness arises concerning their relative knowledge and expertise. At the beginning of this extract, as P holds a piece of a certain herbal medicine, he states that some people mistake it for another kind called *haak phang khii*,[12] but in fact he knows that it is from a plant called *kok sii din*. In the section of interest to us here, Ka then begins with an assertion that the herb known as *haak phang khii* is plentiful (or 'not lacking' as the idiom goes) and is on his way to stating *where* it is plentiful (line 13), but P begins talking and names the place in line 15: 'Vang Phêêng Weir'. This is confirmed or at least accepted in line 17 by Ka. Here we are interested in line 18, spoken by P, which ties back to Ka's utterance in line 13. Speaker Ka had used the expression *bòø qùt2* 'not lacking' in making an assertion about the herb known as *haak phang khii*, and this expression is picked up in line 18, though this time – critically – with the addition of the factive perfective particle *lèq1*. By adding the particle, P carries out the double-barreled action we have seen in the above examples: on the one hand, he is fully agreeing with what his interlocutor has said, while on the other hand he is making it explicit that he has a greater authority to have said it.

---

[12] In the recording, it is not entirely clear that the speaker says *haak phang khii* as opposed to some other medicine; hence the brackets around the words in the transcript here. This does not detract from the point being made here.

His 'agreeing' utterance in line 18 therefore has a 'confirming' character (though of course he had not been asked for confirmation).

(14) 020727a:427

09 P: laang2 khon2 khaw3   vaai (haak4 phang2 khii5)
       some person 3PL.BARE say plant sp.
       Some people, they say (it's haak phang khii),

10   vaai san4. bòø mèènı
       say thus NEG be.so
       (they) say. (That's) not so.

11   qanø-nii4 kok2 sii2 din3 [qanø-niø qaø
       CLF-THIS plant sp.   CLF-this PCL
       This is kok sii din, this.

12 Ka: [haak4 phang2 khii5
                              plant sp.
                              Hak phang khii

13   kaø   bòø qùt2   juuı [thèèw3-
       TLNK   NEG lacking LOC area
       is plentiful, at the area of-

14 P: [qee5
                              yeah

15   kaø   cangı vaaı faaj3 vang2 phêêng2 faaj3
       TLNK so   say weir VP   weir
       Like (I) said, Vang Phêêng Weir, whatever weir,

16   ñang3 qooj4
       what INTJ
       oy.

17 Ka: m5
       Mm.

18	P:	bòø	qùt2	lèqı,	faaj3	qanø	nanø	naø
		NEG	lacking	FAC.PRF	weir	CLF	that	TPC

(It's) not lacking, that weir

A second example (15) of the same pattern is from a conversation between K and S, two men living in neighbouring houses in the same village. Again, there is a certain competitiveness in the air, with K and S disagreeing as to whether certain rural roads around their village are presently navigable. The condition of rural roads is a pervasive topic of discussion and monitoring, as they are always changing because of weather and traffic conditions. In lines 31–33, K is offering evidence from his own recent experience to support his claim that a certain route is difficult to navigate because it is too sandy. S provides what looks like a solution to this in line 34, by stating that it would be easy to take a route that passes through a village called 'Kilometer 40'. K's next turn (in line 36) repeats the key information – 'enter (at) Kilometer 40' – yet adds the final particle *lèqı*, as if this were a kind of confirmation or more specific statement of what the prior speaker had just said (even though it is identical with it). The effect is to bring about the target action: agreeing, yet while claiming greater authority to make the assertion.[13] And through the specific tool chosen for this action, a collateral effect is that the sequence is closed down by virtue of the basic semantics of the particle.

(15) 030806a:242

31	K:	pajø	phèèı	khaw5	kuu3	paj3	hanø	lèqı
		go	distribute	rice	1SG.BARE	go	TPC.DIST	FAC.PRF

(I went) to distribute rice, I went (to that place)

32		cangı	vaaı	man2	pên3	thaang2	khiø-saaj2
		thus	say	3SG.BARE	be	path	sand

Therefore, (that's why I) said it was a sand road.

---

[13] Clearly this is not, in surface terms, an agreement to an *assessment*, but rather to an assertion. This does not, however, detract from the essential function of this format: agreeing while claiming epistemic authority.

33   [vaang1   hanø
          time   TPC.DIST
          That time.

34 S: [maa2   phii4   maa2   phii4   lak2   sii4-sip2
          come   DEM.PROX   come   DEM.PROX   km   40
          Come here come here, Km 40,

35   phii4   sabaaj3
          DEM.PROX   easy
          here easy.

36 K: khaw5 lak2 sii1-sip2 niø   lèq1
          enter km   40   TPC   FAC.PRF
          It is indeed at Km 40 that (you) enter.

In these examples, we have shown how Lao speakers conventionally construct a K+ second assessment by exploiting a lexico-grammatical resource that is characteristic of one of the language's basic organizational properties: final particles (Enfield 2007a: Chapter 4). The particular format chosen – the factive perfective particle *lèq1* – is well-fitted to this function because of its source in a perfective aspectual meaning, along the lines of 'finished'. This lends it an air of 'shutting down' a sequence of interaction.

Conclusion

Our comparative case study shows how three very different languages from three corners of the world provide their speakers with different resources for constructing a common type of social action in interaction: agreeing with what someone just said. These actions – saying things and agreeing with what others say – are crucially implicated in the way members of our language-using species affiliate with one another and thus display solidarity. These linguistically mediated actions are central to our sense of having a common outlook with someone or some group, and hence are central to forming and maintaining alliances and relationships (Enfield 2013).

We have shown that each of the languages discussed provides sufficient tools for carrying out the specific social action we have characterized as a K+ second assessment – i.e., agreeing with what someone just said while conveying that one has greater authority to say it – yet because of the particular tools conventionally chosen for that action, each language brings the action about in a distinct way. This is the third sense of linguistic relativity that we propose: differences in language-specific structures available to different speech communities give rise to differences in the ways that specific social actions are enchronically effected, thereby changing how these actions play out in sequences of social interaction. We have argued that these consequential differences are the outcome of collateral effects arising from properties of the linguistic structures that serve as tools for carrying out the target social action, and that are unavoidably introduced when the structure is selected.

To study these linguistically relative collateral effects, there are two possible points of focus. First we can focus on nuances of meaning in different language strategies. For example, we can compare the Creole case, in which the agreement format treats a prior move as if it had been a question, with the Lao case, in which the particle *lèqı* draws on the semantics of factivity and perfectivity and by this comes to express finality of the agreement turn in interactional and pragmatic terms. Such effects can be subtle. But because they are necessarily cumulative and combinatorial, and because every social action is necessarily tooled by the particular semiotic resources of the language in question, we contend that these subtle effects will result in substantial differences in the ways that general patterns of interaction are inflected (see also Levinson 2005; Schegloff 2006; Sidnell 2007a, 2007b, 2009a, 2009b).

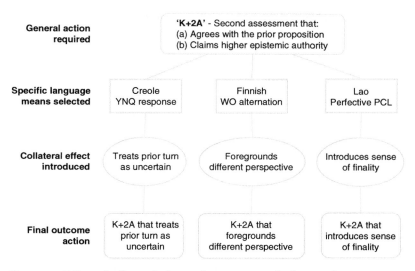

General action required	'K+2A' - Second assessment that: (a) Agrees with the prior proposition (b) Claims higher epistemic authority		
Specific language means selected	Creole YNQ response	Finnish WO alternation	Lao Perfective PCL
Collateral effect introduced	Treats prior turn as uncertain	Foregrounds different perspective	Introduces sense of finality
Final outcome action	K+2A that treats prior turn as uncertain	K+2A that foregrounds different perspective	K+2A that introduces sense of finality

Figure 5.1 Collateral effects of selecting language-specific formats for carrying out a general type of social action 'K-plus Agreeing Second Assessment'. To carry out a certain action, a speaker has no option but to select some language-specific means for doing it; these different means introduce different effects in each language, resulting in different final outcomes.

This is especially clear in the second possible point of focus for studying linguistically relative collateral effects, namely the consequences of a particular action format or practice for subsequent talk. We see this in the comparison of Lao and Creole second assessments, on the one hand, with Finnish VS-formatted second assessments on the other. While the former are implicative of sequence closure, indeed they seem to suggest insistence or having the last word, the VS-formatted second assessments of Finnish imply different perspectives and as a result may be topic-elaborating.

To summarize our findings, it may help to visualize the phenomenon of collateral effects in action, as shown in Figure 5.1.

The figure illustrates how a general action type is conventionally approached in distinct ways in the three languages, in terms of the lexico-syntactic resources that each language provides as a vehicle for that action. Because of the different properties of the language-specific vehicles, each language enables speakers to hit the same broad target, but never quite in the same way: different collateral effects are introduced.

The question of linguistic relativity continues to be debated in current anthropology, attracting as much interest as ever (Leavitt 2011; Everett 2013; Enfield 2015). Amid continued debate and further studies concerning the consequences of language diversity for cognition, and for cultural context, we have tried to formulate a new, third direction for this work. Our third locus for linguistic relativity can be found in the enchronic context of social action as carried out through talk in everyday interaction. Because such social action is done with the tools that our languages provide, and because these tools are structurally overdetermined through their rich meanings and multiple functions, the conventionalized selection of such tools will have language-specific collateral effects on the final nature of the action.

On this view, the language you speak makes a difference for the social actions you can perform. The language-specific vehicle or means for an action – even where that action is a general goal or end that we expect people will want to pursue in any cultural context – will shape the action as a function of the structures it introduces. Our case study suggests ways in which a general target action type can be tooled in different ways by different languages (and indeed, where such tooling cannot be avoided) because of structural differences in the language-specific vehicles for conventionally carrying out that action. By selecting a certain lexico-syntactic vehicle as a means for achieving social-action ends, speakers unavoidably introduce associated features, thereby introducing the collateral effects we suggest are imported by limitations of lexico-syntactic resources for the construction of social action through primarily linguistic turns-at-talk – which, by virtue of being linguistic, must be in some language. This means not only that differences in language structure are associated with differences in patterns of thought or cultural context but that differences in language structure lead to linguistically relative collateral effects that lead, in turn, to differences in our very possibilities for social agency.

∾

SIX

Natural Meaning

Royal wedding, Kate and William, 29.04.2011 (AofC = Archbishop of Canterbury)

AofC: William. Arthur. Philip Louis. (0.4) wilt thou have this woman to thy wedded wife, (0.2) to live together according to God's law in the holy estate of matrimony. (0.4) Wilt thou love her. (.) comfort her. honour and keep her. (.) in sickness and in health (.) and forsaking all other keep thee only onto her (.) so long as ye both shall live?

W: I will

(0.6)

AofC: Catherine Elizabeth. wilt thou have this man to thy wedded husband. (.) to live together according to God's la:w in the holy estate of matrimony. (.) Wilt thou love him, comfort him, honour and keep him. in sickness and in health. (.) and forsaking all other keep thee only onto him. so long as ye both shall live.

K: I will

We have argued in this book that social action is built using the tools of language. As we noted in the last chapter, the languages of the world provide greatly diverse meanings and structures, and so it should follow that people who speak different languages build social actions in fundamentally different ways. Our comparative case study showed that the language-specific tools used to realize a single action introduce collateral effects and in this way give the action a local spin or inflection. Is our potential for action a function of the language we speak? Could the human potential for social action be linguistically relative? The answer, we proposed, is yes.

In the form of linguistic relativity that we have indicated, action in interaction is subject to language-specific inflections which, cumulatively, result in significant differences across languages. Our goal in the present chapter is to emphasize that this does not entail a position of extreme or unbridled relativism. The relativity arising from collateral effects is just one of the countervailing forces that shape the design of action in interaction. Another shaping force is the universality of natural meaning, by which we mean interpretation grounded in iconic and indexical principles, not arbitrary conventions (see Haiman 1985). In this chapter we focus on this second force, a force towards universality. Our case study relates to the systems that languages possess for answering polar questions (or yes–no questions; see Stivers and Enfield 2010). In this pragmatic domain, we will argue that the form-to-meaning mappings that we observe across languages are based on nonarbitrary principles and are likely to imply universality of meaning patterning.

The Adjacency Pair

Before we proceed, let us review an important preliminary to our argument. A universal feature of language is the presence of *adjacency pairs* in conversational dialogue (see, *inter alia*, Schegloff and Sacks 1973; Sacks, Schegloff, and Jefferson 1974; Stivers et al. 2009; Sidnell 2010a). An adjacency pair is a sequence of two utterances, in which the first (called a *first pair part*), spoken by Person A, sets up a strong normative expectation (or 'conditional relevance') for the immediate production of an appropriate or 'fitted' second utterance (called a *second pair part*), spoken by Person B.

Perhaps the clearest example of an adjacency pair is the kind of question–answer sequences we focus on in this chapter. If Emma asks

Are you still taking your shots? and Lottie replies *Yeah*, this is an adjacency pair. An answer from Lottie was expected, and if she had stayed silent, the answer would have been, as Schegloff (1968) put it, 'officially absent'. The first utterance in an adjacency pair activates a powerful set of norms within which a second speaker must act. Even if she remains silent, this will be understood in relation to the normative expectation that she should have answered. So in an important sense she does not, in fact, have the option of 'not acting', as in that particular moment almost any behaviour she produces will be read as a response.

In these tightly paired utterance sequences, we can recognize two positions. A question is a *first-position* element, and an answer is a *second-position* element. These two positions (and others based on these such as third and fourth) have important consequences for language structure, yet they have been mostly overlooked in linguistic typology despite their utility in grammatical analysis (cf. Gipper 2011; Enfield 2013:71).

To preview our discussion, it can be observed that these positions exhibit a basic structural asymmetry: whereas a first-position utterance (such as a question) initiates a sequence of action and activates a set of norms, a second-position utterance is, inherently, more reactive. In this chapter we are asking what resources languages provide for second-position speakers to 'act' rather than simply 'react' and so to exert their own agency (see also Thompson, Fox, and Couper-Kuhlen 2015). In the background is the question of whether the differences between languages make a difference to how this might be done (see Chapter 5).

Responding to Polar Questions

We now turn to a specific issue in the analysis of question–answer sequences. How do people answer polar questions in different languages? The received view in linguistic typology is that there are 'three different answering systems': '(i) yes/no systems, (ii) agree/disagree systems, and (iii) echo systems' (König and Siemund 2007:320). The difference between types (i) and (ii) has to do with the interpretation of polarity in relation to confirmation and disconfirmation. Suppose I ask, *He doesn't have a phone there does he?* If you want to confirm that he does not have a phone, you would say 'No' in English (*No he doesn't have one*) but 'Yes' in Japanese (*Yes it's true he doesn't have one*). But despite this important difference in the rules of interpretation, systems of type (i) and (ii) are identical in that they answer polar questions with a kind of interjection that is entirely indexical, getting its meaning solely from the content of the question to which it responds. For both 'No' and 'Yes', in our example, one has to look back at the question to know what the response actually means.

A very different kind of system is implied by type (iii). König and Siemund (2007:321) repeat a widely made claim, that in an 'echo system', 'no special answer words at all can be found.' The strong implication is that some languages have no forms for 'yes' or 'no' (though there is no evidence to support this oft-made claim). They state that 'Welsh and Finnish are among the languages in our sample possessing such an echo system' (ibid.), implying that these two languages have *only* this echo system. But in fact both of these languages have forms that mean 'yes' and 'no' (see Jones 1999 on Welsh and Sorjonen 2001 on Finnish). They make 'echo' type answers available alongside the interjection option, just as English does. The point is that these 'types' do not refer to distinct types of language, as is often implied. As far as we are aware, every language has both types of system – interjection and 'echo' – though of course there may be differences in usage and distribution of the alternatives.[1] It appears, then, that when people want to answer a polar

---

[1] See Enfield et al. (2017), for an analysis that also includes another oft-cited case of a language without an interjection option: Brazilian Portuguese. This language has *sim* for 'Yes', but it is often said that people 'never say it', instead opting for a kind of repetition strategy. The reality appears to be that *sim* is used but rarely. It may be that other interjection strategies are widely used. Like *uh-huh* and *mm* in English, some forms are overlooked by analysts because of

question, no matter which language they are speaking, they have the option of using an interjection strategy or an echo strategy. Let us consider these possibilities more closely.

Interjection Strategy

The interjection strategy for answering polar questions involves the use of words such as English *yes* and *no*. These are interjections in the sense defined in traditional grammar (e.g., Bloomfield 1933), that is, words that may stand alone as full utterances in themselves. We include in the set of interjections not only words like *yes* and *no*, but variants such as *yeah, yep, nah, nope*, as well as marked terms with related but more specific meanings like *absolutely (not)* or *of course (not)*, and forms that are less likely to be listed in formal linguistic descriptions, including vocalizations like *mm*, and visible responses such as head nods. The set of items that qualify as interjections for the purpose of answering polar questions is large and varied. All languages will have a set of forms, with non-identical alternatives. The precise meaning, function, and distribution of these will differ from language to language. Traditional grammatical treatments account for the meanings in terms of matching response type to question type (e.g., German *ja* versus *doch*, or the English versus Japanese system for confirming a negative question) or in terms of relative politeness or formality (see Vietnamese *ừ* vs. *dạ* vs. *vâng*), but we do not know of an account for why a respondent confirms a question with *yes* in one context and *mm hm* or *uh huh* or nodding in other contexts.

Repetition Strategy

The repetition strategy for answering polar questions involves repeating part or all of a question with adjustments resulting from a shift of deictic

their highly informal or non-standard character. Enfield et al. (2017) aims to settle the matter with reference to comparative data from language usage.

centre: e.g., *Did you eat my cake?* may elicit *I ate your cake* as a repetition strategy for giving a confirming answer. This kind of modification in repetition is trivial, but there are many more kinds of transformation upon a question that may be done within the repetition strategy (cf. Stivers and Hayashi 2010). An important aspect of this strategy is transformation by means of replacement of full nominal forms with pro-forms. Thus, alternative repetitional answers to *I ate your cake* would include *I ate it*, in which the object noun phrase is replaced with the pronoun *it*, and *I did*, in which the entire verb phrase is replaced with the pro-form *do*. In addition, a repetition type response can be transformed in further ways by the addition of elements like an emphatic auxiliary verb (*I did eat your cake*) and other kinds of adverbs or particles (*I sure as hell did*). Despite all of this variation and expressive possibility, these are all cases of what we want to call a repetition strategy of answering.

So this is our starting point. All languages provide a choice between two options: an interjection strategy (such as *yes* in English) and a repetition strategy (e.g., repeating a verb or verb phrase). A null hypothesis would be that these two strategies have the same meaning (merely confirming or disconfirming) and that they occur in free variation. But we argue that the two options carry a subtle difference in meaning, that this difference is due to their natural semiotics, and therefore that the meaning difference should be apparent in all languages. Interjection strategies carry no inherent propositional content: to understand the meaning being conveyed, the interpreter must consult the question (spoken by a different person, in first position). Therefore, interjection answers should universally convey the idea that the answerer generally accepts the terms in which the question was framed. By contrast, repetition strategies, at least in their fullest form, independently convey the propositional content of what is being confirmed. Therefore, they should universally convey the idea that the answerer is being more assertive, taking greater 'ownership' over what is being said in the utterance that ostensibly is asserting agreement or confirmation. There may, of course, be local inferential meanings ranging from resistance (or 'pushing back') to independent epistemic access and so on (see Hayano 2011, 2013). More generally however, interjections are wholly dependent upon and indexical of the turns to which they respond and as such they are intrinsically identifiable as *responses*. By contrast, repetition strategies allow their speakers to reassert their own independent agency in second position, because repetition strategies are not intrinsically marked as responsive.

Key to our argument here is the observation that these alternative response forms are not distributed randomly across different sequential contexts. To preview our analysis based on conversation in English, we will show that interjection confirmations are typically used in response to simple requests for confirmation (such as candidate answer questions), whereas various repeat formats appear specialized to contexts in which the question recipient attempts to reassert agency or priority in a context where that has been in some sense challenged by the questioning turn.[2]

Analysis

Interjection Confirmation

Consider first the use of an interjection to confirm a polar question in English. One common context for this usage is in response to what is described as a 'candidate answer question' such as in the following.[3]

---

[2] For this analysis we draw on a large collection (200+) of polar questions and their responses drawn from the Newport Beach corpus of recordings available here: www.talkbank.org /browser/index.php?url=CABank/Jefferson/NB/

[3] We define *candidate answer question* rather more narrowly than Pomerantz (1988) who introduced the term. For us a candidate answer question canonically takes the form of [wh-question] + [candidate answer] or simply [candidate answer] with the question elided. Examples we discuss here include: 'How old's 'e gunnuh be.' + 'Fifty six?' (NB II:3:r), 'What' + 'that fungus?' (NB II:3:r), '∅' + 'That Revlo:n?' (NB II:3:r), 'Wt's the name' + 'i-San Juan Hi:lls.huh?=' (NB 1.1).

(1) NB II:3:r(10)
01   Emma: How old's 'e gunnuh be.
02   (0.7)
03   Emma: Fifty ↑six?
04   Lottie: Ye:ah.
05   (0.3)
06   Emma: Ah'll be darn.

Here a wh-question establishes what is being asked about and, after a delay of 0.7 seconds, the candidate answer 'fifty-six' is offered up for confirmation. Confirmation is accomplished by a simple interjection token 'Ye:ah'.

In the next example (2), Emma first asks 'How is yer artherahtis', but before Lottie can answer appends the polar question, 'yih still tak'n sho:ts?'. In her response Lottie first confirms the polar question with a simple interjection before providing a response to the wh-question which preceded it. She thus treats the polar question as amenable to straightforward, direct confirmation (see Sacks 1987).

(2) NB II:3:r(12)
01   Lottie: Ye[a:h.]
02   Emma: [Yeh a]t's goo:d. u.-How is yer artherahtis,
03   yih still tak'n sho:ts?
04   Lottie: ↑Ye:a:h u- [↑w u l: i]t's: ↑i-it's ↓awri:::ght
05   Emma: [°°Ah-ha°°]
06   Lottie: <I mean:=it's e- ↓uh::: (0.2) it ut hurts once'n
07   a [wh i :l e] but
08   Emma: [Mm hm]
09   (.)
10   Lottie: it's oka:y.=

Where the question is negatively formatted confirmation is, of course, effected by use of the negative interjection token *no* as in example (3):

(3) NB I:1:r(3)
01   Guy: He dun'av a phone over there dud'e?
02   Jon: No:.

Other variants include the tokens *uh huh* and *mm hm* as in the following (another Wh+candidate):

(4) NB I:1:r(7)
```
01   Guy:   Wt's the name i-San Juan Hi:lls.huh?=
02   Jon:   =hUh huh? .hhhh
03          (0.6)
04          I have the Hunningtin Seacli:ff?
```

Across all the interjection examples, confirmation is treated as a simple matter and, once the question is confirmed, either the sequence is concluded by a third position closing turn or the participants move directly to other matters as in (4). Thus, the interjection accepts the terms of the question as posed. Notice also that in each of the cases above, the question is constructed so as to convey a relatively high degree of certainty. For instance, *He dun'av a phone over there dud'e?* conveys relative certainty as compared to an alternate possible form such as *Does he have a phone over there?* Lee (2015) notes that, whereas 'interrogative forms . . . , indexing the questioner's unknowing stance, tend to be treated as inviting elaboration that will inform the questioner', formats that encode 'questioner's knowing stance, tend to invite confirmation of the matter at hand and possible sequence closure . . . A minimal, type-conforming token alone is considered adequate, as the questioner claims to be knowledgeable to some degree through the form of question.'

To summarize, unelaborated interjection responses treat confirmation as a simple matter, are indexically dependent on the question to which they respond, accept the terms of the question as unproblematic, and maximize sequence progressivity. Not surprisingly, then, they are commonly produced in response to questions with a 'shallow' epistemic gradient, that is, where the questioner conveys relative certainty about the matters asked about (see also Heritage and Raymond 2012:183).[4]

---

[4] See also examples from institutional interaction. For instance, when Guy calls the golf course to schedule a time to play part of the interaction runs off like this:

Desk: 'Foursome?', Guy: 'Yah'.

Another frequently occurring pattern is one in which an interjection token is followed by a repeat. The following examples in (5) to (7) are illustrative.

(5) NB IV:11:r(1)

```
01   Emma:    Ah did↑ ju[ge:tch e ]r paper this: morning=
02   Gladys:         [ Ahshh ]
03   Emma:    =it wz ou:t'n [fron'v a:r pl↓a:ce.=
04   Gladys:                [m-
05            =Yes dear ah di↓:d.
06   Emma:    Bud took't over on the porch he didn'know
07            whether yih w'r u:p.h
08   Gladys:  u-Well thank you yes I did
```

(6) NB I:1:r(2)

```
01   Guy:   Wut about dat SAN JUAN ↑HILLS down 'ere.
02          Yuh think we c'get on 'ere?
03          (.)
04   Jon:   Ye:s I think so:,
```

(7) NB I:1:r(3)

```
01   Guy:   Is Cliff dow:n by any chance?=diyuh ↑°know°?
02          (0.3)
03   Jon:   ↑Ha:h?
04   Guy:   I:ss uh: Bro:wn down-e?
05          (.)
06   Jon:   Yeah he's do:wn,
07   Guy:   Think he'd like to [↑go?
08   Jon:                      [Played golf with im yesterday
09          et San Clemente.
10   Guy:   Yih di:[d.hh
11   Jon:          [Uh huh?
12   Guy:   Think he'd like tih go:?
13   Jon:   I: uh,h I don't ↑kno:w, uh:heh heh hu:h huh.hhh
14          Ah(h)'ll I(c) I c'd go by ed see:,
```

We can notice that across these cases, an anaphoric or elliptical repeat of some part of the question is appended to the interjection.

Did you get your paper this morning → (yes dear) I did ∅
You think we can get on there → (yes) I think so
Is Brown down → (yeah) he's down

Each of these questions is recognizably preliminary to some other action, that is, these questions are not asked solely for their own sake. Rather, they are headed somewhere. They project the doing of a next action. For instance in (5) Emma asks whether Gladys got her newspaper which subsequently leads her to explain that it was 'out in front of our place' and that her husband Bud had taken it over. This, then, occasions an appreciation by Gladys in line 08. In (6) Guy asks Jon whether he thinks they might be able get on the San Juan Hills golf course. The question is recognizably leading to the proposal that they play there that afternoon. Finally, in (7), Guy asks Jon if a mutual acquaintance, Brown, 'is down', meaning, it would appear, at his summer house in Newport Beach. This projects a proposal that Brown be invited to play golf with the group thus rounding out a foursome. These questions can be compared with those given as examples (1)–(4) which do not appear to be preliminary to some other business and thus do not project sequence expansion. Rather, as is most obvious in the case of candidate answer questions, these questions are asked to address some immediate, interactionally relevant issue and are not preliminary to something else. A corollary of this, it seems, is that whereas the questions in (1)–(4) are constructed using the format [declarative] + [tag] or as candidate answer questions, those given as examples (5)–(8) are constructed using an interrogative format. These questions thus convey a steeper epistemic gradient than those in (1)–(4).

It would appear, then, that by the addition of a repeat the recipient addresses some contingency of action relevance that extends beyond a mere request for information (see Schegloff 2007; Raymond 2013; Steensig and Heinemann 2013). So, for instance, in (7) when Guy asks whether 'Brown is down', he is recognizably projecting a proposal that Brown be invited. Jon confirms with 'yeah', but by adding 'he's down' marks this as a strict conveyance of information and hints that there may be a problem with the proposal that has been projected. Notice, then, that when Guy follows up with 'Think he'd like to go', Jon does not answer; rather, he remarks that he played golf with him the day before, thereby accounting for how he knows that Brown is down while at the same time suggesting that, given that he just played yesterday, he may not want to play again today. And when Guy asks again whether Brown would like to go, Jon refuses to answer, responding instead with 'I don't know' and 'I could go by and see'.

The [interjection] + [repeat] format appears particularly fitted to confirm questions with a relatively steep epistemic gradient and is used where the recipient means to address both the question posed and the action for which that question is the vehicle (see, *inter alia*, Raymond 2003; Heritage and Raymond 2012; Keevallik 2010; Lee 2012).

Repeat Confirmations

We can compare such cases with those in which confirmation is accomplished by a straight repeat. As Heritage and Raymond (2012: 186) write, while

repetitive responses remain indexically tied to the questions to which they respond, they differ from straightforward anaphoric yes–no responses. Specially, they resist the field of constraint exerted by the question in three respects: (i) they modify the terms of the question by confirming, rather than simply affirming, the propositional content of the prior yes–no question; (ii) they exert agency with respect to those terms, asserting more authoritative rights over the information at issue, than the questioner had already conceded through the design of the question; and (iii) relative to yes–no responses, they are associated with sequence expansion.

Repeat confirmations (with no interjection token) occur in a restricted set of sequential contexts. Specifically, we find this strategy used in the following environments:

a. In response to a first assessment formatted as a polar question (see Heritage and Raymond 2005).
b. In response to a newsmark formatted as a polar question such as (8):

(8) NB:II:4r(10), 5:50
01   Nancy: =I din't get home til (.) .hhhh two las'night I
02   met a very:,h very n:i:ce ↓gu:y.
03   Emma: Did(.)ju↓::.=
04   Nancy: =I: rill↑y did. through the↑:se: frien:ds of mi↑:ne?h

c. In response to the formulation of a prior telling formatted as a polar question (see also allusion confirmations, Schegloff 1996).[5]

We will consider this last environment in more detail in what follows. Essentially, what we see in this subset of cases is that a first speaker is engaged in an extended telling towards which she adopts either a positive or a negative stance. Where this comes to a point of recognizable completion, the recipient produces a polar question in which she asks about some aspect of the state of affairs described by formulating an upshot of the telling. This turn is designed as a declaratively formatted inference to which *huh?* is appended, thus making it a polar question. In response to this, the initial teller responds with a repeat formatted confirmation. Examples (9) and (10) are illustrative:

---

[5] Use of repetition to confirm a polar question is not common in English conversation. Indeed, use of this strategy appears to be linked to a rather specific set of interactional outcomes such as we describe above or such as those that Schegloff (1996) describes as 'confirming an allusion'.

(9) NB:II:2r(18)

```
01   Nancy:   [L e t -] I : ] hu [n:No: I haf to: uh
02            call Roul's mother,h I told'er I:'d call'er
03            this morning I [ gotta letter ] from'er en
04   Emma:                   [°(Uh huh. )°]
05   Nancy:   .hhhhhh A:nd uhm
06            (1.0)
07   Nancy:   .tch u -So: she in the letter she said if you
08            ca:n why (.) yihknow call me Saturday morning
09            en I jst haven't h [ .hhhh ]
10   Emma:                       [°Mm h]m:°=
11   Nancy:   ='T's like takin a beating.
12            (0.2)
13   Nancy:   kh[hh ↑hnhh hnh] -hnh - [hnh
14   Emma: →    [ °Mm: : :,° ]        [No one heard a wo:rd
15            hah,
16   Nancy:   >Not a word,<
17            (0.2)
18   Nancy:   Hah ah,
19            (0.2)
20   Nancy:   n:Not (.) not a word,h
21            (.)
22   Nancy:   Not et all, except Roul's mother gotta call
```

(10) NB:II:5r(9-10), 5:50

```
01   Emma:    So[u It's terr:]ible up
02   Lottie:    [°O h : : : °]
03            (.)
04   Emma:    ↑It's TERR:IBLE up .hhh -we lie: - (0.4) We
05            absolutely lie: star:k naked on the be:d,
06            (0.2)
07   Emma:    .hh with ↑MAYbe a sheet o:n about two
08            uh' ↓clock.
09            (0.6)
10   Lottie: → It's that ho:t h[u : h ? ]
11   Emma:                     [Tha:t's] that ho:t.
12            (0.4)
13   Emma:    Believe it er no:t an' en we got the
14            air conditioning=
```

In (9) Nancy tells Emma that she must call the mother of her husband, Roul, who has apparently run off and cut all ties with his family (wife, children, mother). Nancy expresses some reluctance to make the call reporting that it is like 'taking a beating'. Emma's question in lines 14–15 ('No one heard a <u>wo</u>:rd hah') formulates an inference based on Nancy's just prior talk – specifically from the facts that Nancy's mother-in-law wants her to call, that Nancy feels obligated to do so, and from the fact that Nancy describes the situation as 'like taking a beating' Emma can surmise, it seems, that no one has heard anything from Roul. Emma's question takes the form of an extreme case formulation (Pomerantz 1986) to which the tag 'huh?' is appended, thus leaving Nancy very little room to upgrade or expand. She manages the situation by use of a repeat formatted confirmation which itself is first repeated and subsequently reformatted as the elliptical 'not at all' before being qualified with 'except Roul's mother got a call' (see Sacks 1987).

In (10) Emma is telling her sister Lottie how hot it has been where she lives (not Newport Beach). Initially she describes the heat as 'terrible' but then goes on to detail that she and her husband 'absolutely lie stark naked on the bed' and, after Lottie fails to respond, expands by saying 'with maybe a sheet on about 2 o'clock'. At this point Lottie asks 'It's that hot, huh?' and Emma confirms with a repeat formatted '(that's) that hot'.

In both these cases the question comes in response to a telling that describes a somewhat extraordinary state of affairs – extreme heat in (10), extreme negligence by a husband in (9). These descriptions are thus designed to elicit an expression of affiliative stance from the recipient. We can see how these formulation questions do that by conveying some upshot of the telling using a [declarative] + [tag] form that claims a 'knowing stance'. In these cases, then, the recipient of a telling ends up authoring and animating an upshot of that telling. As such, confirmation by repetition can be seen as a reassertion of primary rights to talk about what is, after all, the initial teller's own experience. At the same time the original teller, by confirming with a repeat rather than an interjection, conveys their own (emotional) involvement – indeed asserts it – in the telling (see Goffman 1957).[6]

These cases thus establish a use of repetition to confirm a telling-recipient's formulation of upshot as a practice. We can now consider a deviant case in which in precisely such a situation, a speaker confirms with an interjection rather than a repeat and the participants orient to this as problematic and worthy of sanction.

As Heritage and Raymond note (2012:187), 'there are actions in which an affirmative type-conforming response can be too acquiescent, and imply insufficient agency and commitment to a course of action being assented to'. In example (11), Jim has asked Frank about the waves at the beach (lines 01–02) and after Frank estimates their size (line 04) Jim offers the assessment 'Christ thirty feet' (in the previous call there is mention made of a news report about this).[7] A first indication of trouble comes when Frank initiates repair of this assessment at line 10 and when Jim asks if the waves come 'all the way up to the houses'. Frank disconfirms, indicating that the waves extend just to where the sidewalk ends. Frank thereby minimizes a possible news item that Jim has treated as something potentially tellable/assessable (see Sidnell 2012a for discussion).

(11) NB: III:2r(4-5)

```
01   Jim:     Bye now .h Ho:w u-how big er those waves
02            down theh.
03            (0.4)
04   Frank:   Oh:: about (.) thirty foot I guess
```

---

[6] Goffman (1957:49) writes 'as Adam Smith argued in his *Theory of the Moral Sentiments*, the individual must phrase his own concerns and feelings and interests in such a way as to make these maximally usable by the others as a source of appropriate involvement; and this major obligation of the individual *qua* interactant is balanced by his right to expect that others present will make some effort to stir up their sympathies and place them at his command'.

[7] These recordings were made in the summer months of 1968. From May until August the pacific coast of the United States was hit by five named storms which cumulatively resulted in one of the most extreme weather systems in recorded history for this region. See http://en .wikipedia.org/wiki/1968_Pacific_hurricane_season

```
05              (1.7)
06   Jim:       Chris[t th i rty fee]:t.
07   Frank:          [Big enough::]
08              (.)
09   Jim:       Thet's[hh
10   Frank:           [He::h?
11   Jim:       Thirty fee(h)eet,[·hh Is]
12   Frank:                      [↑Ye:h.]
13   Jim:       Is it all a'way up tih the houssiz?
14              (0.5)
15   Frank:     Oh: ↓no:. ↓No it's jis comes uup (.)Yihknow
16              where the: -uh(p) (0.4) Uh you ben down here
17              before['avenche.]
18   Jim:              [ Y a a h .]
19   Frank:     Wheh the sidewalk is?
20   Jim:       Ye:ah?
21   Frank:     Whur it ends,
22              (.)
23   Jim:       Goes[all the way ] up there?]
24   Frank:         [They c'm up]   tuh the:,h Yea:h.
25   Jim: →     Je:sus Christ must be so:methin uh[:?
26   (F):                                         [(.tch)
27   Frank:     °↑mnYe:ah,° hhh ((wearily))
28              Gits pretty hh (.) .hh[hh
29   Jim:                             [Don't sound so
30              (h)amp(h)itious=
31   Frank:     =[.ehh
32   Jim:       =[fer Ch(h)rise'sake [(h)ih suh.hh]=
33   Frank:                          [ Y  e  :  h ]=
34   Jim:       =sou' l(h)i'yuh k(h)uh g(h)o tuh sleep'n the
35              pho(h)one.
36   Frank:     eheh huh [heh heh [huh huh-eh .hhh
37   Jim:                [heh     [heh
38   Frank:     I jis woke ↑U:P huh heh heh ↑hih
```

Notice then that when Jim produces the polar question, 'Je:sus Christ must be so:methin uh:?' at line 25, he is apparently pursuing a more emphatic response from Frank. Frank, however, responds with a simple interjection confirmation (at line 27). Now although there are clearly other factors that contribute to Jim's hearing of this 'yeah', it is noteworthy that Jim treats the interjection response as warranting sanction saying, 'Don't sound so ambitious'[8] and going on to say that Frank sounds as though he is going to go to sleep on the phone.

Let us digress briefly on the matter of action formation in this case. As Jefferson noted in the transcript with the annotation 'wearily', there's something in the prosody of the way Frank produces this token that suggests lack of involvement. Some commentators on this analysis have suggested that this fact undermines the strength of our argument, since it might be the prosody to which Jim is responding with sanction rather than the choice of an interjection token instead of a more affirmative form of confirmation. But this is to treat action as a kind of 'triggering' phenomenon in which single features of an utterance convey the action import of the whole. As we argue in Chapters 1 and 2, we believe that this is implausible. We argue for an approach in which actions result from an orchestration of practices (of position and composition). From our perspective, the intonation that Jefferson noted with 'wearily' is actually and merely consistent with Frank's selection of the interjection token – together and along with other features of the talk they provide for the inference that Frank is emotionally uninvolved, and it is this that serves as the warrant for Jim's sanction in following turns. A final point here has to do with the particular way in which Jim formulates the complainable matter – Jim scolds Frank by saying 'don't *sound* so ambitious' and 'you *sound* like you're going to go to sleep on the phone'. Does this reference to the sound perhaps reveal an orientation to prosody as opposed to lexical formulation/form selection? We think not. Thus, although there are cases in which a speaker, describing the way something sounds, seems principally concerned with prosody and

---

[8] This is an odd choice of words; perhaps the speaker was searching for the more idiomatic 'Don't sound so enthusiastic'.

intonation, there are others in which this is clearly not the case. Examples (12) and (13) illustrate the first and second possibility respectively:

(12) TG - Opening
```
01    Ava:   H'llo:?
02    Bee:   hHi:,
03    Ava:   Hi:?
04    Bee:   hHowuh you:?
05    Ava:   Oka:::y?hh=
06    Bee:   =Good.=Yihs[ou:nd  ] hh
07    Ava:              [<I wan]'dih know if yih got a-uh:m
08           wutchimicawllit. A:: pah(hh)khing place
09           °th's mornin'.˙hh
10    Bee:   A pa:rking place,
11    Ava:   Mm hm,
12           (0.4)
13    Bee:   Whe:re.
14    Ava:   t! Oh: just anypla(h)ce? I wz jus' kidding yuh.
15    Bee:   Nno?=
16    Ava:   =[(°No).]
17    Bee:   =[W h y ]whhat'sa mattuh with y-
18           Yih sou[nd HA:PPY,] hh
19    Ava:          [  Nothing. ]
20    Ava:   u- I sound ha:p[py?]
21    Bee:                  [Yee]uh.
22           (0.3)
23    Ava:   No:,
24    Bee:   Nno:?
25    Ava:   No.
26           (0.7)
27    Bee: →˙hh You [sound sorta] cheer[ful? ]
28    Ava:          [°(Any way).]      [˙hh ]
29           How'v you bee:n.
30    Bee:   ˙hh Oh:: survi:ving I guess, hhh!
```

(13) Debbie/Shelley - that's how it sounds
```
42    Debbie:  ↑I just don want you do it jus because Mark's
43             not going cause th[ats just
```

44	Shelley:	[Oh I know.=
45	Debbie:	=that=
46	Shelley:	>°I know°<=
47	Debbie:	=its jus'like you- yaknow:, if you don't wanta do
48		something with like a gi:rlfriend jus cause
49		th's guy:s not goin[g it] would piss me o:ff.
50	Shelley:	[no:.]
51	Shelley:	give me a break.
52	Debbie:	↑well Shelley: that's how it sou::nds.=
53	Shelley:	=w'll a-=
54	Debbie:	=I mean I'm jus telling you how it sou:[nds.
55	Shelley:	[I
56		understand that

Returning to our example (11) above, both in the very fact of sanctioning Frank's response and in the very design of talk that does this, Jim orients to the interjection response as somehow insufficient, indeed, as specifically lacking in agency (i.e., produced as though by someone falling asleep). We speculate that alternative responses such as *oh it's really something* or *it's crazy* would not have attracted such response.

In all the cases of confirmation by repeat, a speaker can be seen to be reclaiming ground, either as the initial author and/or principal of something that has just been animated by another (as in the case of confirming an allusion) or as one who authentically and independently arrives at an assessment to which she finds herself responding. Lee (2012:426) writes along these lines: 'Repetitional responses are thus used to exert and contest epistemic agency over the terms within which the response should be constructed.'

Natural Meaning in Action Formation, Cross-Linguistic Universal Patterning

In our discussion so far about how polar questions are answered, we have suggested that the specific mappings of form to function in the formation of action in this domain are based on non-arbitrary semiotic principles. As we have argued, that *yes* is less agentive than *it is* in response to a question is not a fact that is determined arbitrarily, rather, it is motivated by the natural semiotic properties of the formal options. The options we have described – interjection versus repetition – are available in all languages and are not defined in language-specific terms. This implies that languages other than English should tend to pattern in the same way as English in the linguistic formation of action in this domain. As we have seen in English, an interjection response 'goes along' with terms of the question (Heritage and Raymond 2012), while a repetition tends to 'push back' or convey the agency, authority, ownership, or otherwise special involvement of the confirmer. We propose that there is a natural meaning motivation for this mapping, that is to say, a principle or set of principles for action formation based in universal semiotic principles.

Consider first interjection responses. If John asks *Was it boring?* and Mary answers *Yes*, she is allowing John to be the author and animator of what she's effectively saying (i.e., 'It was boring'). In order to know the content of what Mary's saying by confirming, one would have to consult John's original question. Thus, *yes* (along with other functional equivalent interjections such as head nods and grunts) is *intrinsically a response*, by its very semiotic make-up. This is true of answer interjections and equivalents in any language. As such, to confirm by *Yes* is to go along with a questioner's project by merely indexing it: in our example, Mary is content to let 'boring' be the description, when of course any number of other descriptions may have been possible.

In contrast, if she confirms by repetition (saying *It was boring*, or perhaps *It was*), then, formally, it is as if she had said it independently. One does not need to have heard the question to know what is being asserted. Repetition is thus iconic of 'I say this independently' – again, independent of which language it occurs in, as repetition is a possibility in all languages. One can get the propositional content of what Mary is saying directly from her utterance rather than by consulting something to which it responds. As such, repetition is *not* intrinsically a response and, indeed, it coveys by implicature 'this is not a response' by virtue of its systematic opposition with *Yes*.

Now, as we have seen, this basic, underlying natural meaning of response by repetition is spun out into a wide range of local, inferentially generated meanings. In the cases we have considered above, for example, a repeat can be used to fulfil the 'involvement obligations' associated with being the speaker of a telling.

If this account is correct, we can expect to see a similar distribution in line with this in other languages. Evidence suggests that this is indeed the case. For instance, we find broad support in work on Finnish and Estonian as well as Danish (see, e.g., Sorjonen 2001; Keevallik 2010; Steensig and Heinemann 2013). We also have suggestive evidence from other languages we have worked on, such as Lao and Vietnamese. Let us illustrate with data from Vietnamese.

In Vietnamese, a range of interjection responses are used (varying according to various situational factors) to simply confirm candidate answer questions such as in the following examples:

(14) 6655- 0:24 (Talking about a phone number)

01   C: À thê lại đổi rồi.
          Oh, so she changed again.

02   V: Vâng
          Yes,

(15) 4291 - 4:05 (talking about the model of a car recently purchased)

01   Thuấn: Toyota Maxima á   hả
               Toyota Maxima that huh?
               Toyota maxima huh?

02 Thanh: Ừ
Mm

In contrast to these simple, unmarked, interjection confirmations, repetition responses are associated with some special degree of involvement in, or ownership over, what is being said. So for instance, in the following case (16) T is explaining to H that various members of his extended family do not want to go to Texas (to live). H then voices the inference that T also will not go to live in Texas (using a negative formulation to which is appended the tag / hả/). This is clearly a matter about which T can be expected to have strong feelings, feelings which he may feel it is uniquely his place to articulate. He confirms with a repetition.

(16) 6064 - 26:16

01 T: Ờ, nhưng mà đó, ta thì chắc chưa có đẩy,
Uh, but that, I then sure yet have there,
Uh, but you know, I am quite sure that not yet,

02 gia đình chắc cũng không muốn xuống.
family sure also not want come down.
my family does not want to come down here.

03 Như anh Chung đó kìa, thằng Tước đó kìa,
Like brother Chung that, guy Tước that,
like brother Chung, Tuoc,

04 mấy đứa đâu có chịu đi đâu mà.
those guys do not accept go not that.
they don't want to go.

05 H: không đi hả?
Not go huh?
Not going huh?

06 T: Ờ, khồng đi.
        Uh, not go.
        Uh, no.

In example (17), L is describing to D how she first met the man who would eventually become her husband. According to L, when she first became aware of the man's interest in her she had no idea who he was and thus no idea of what he looked like at all. When D asks 'You didn't know anything?' this is confirmed with a repetition. And when D follows up with 'you didn't know his face?' this is again confirmed with a repetition now with the 'assertive' marker *có* inserted.

(17) 4212

01 Diep: vậy hả? (vậy) mà L khồng biết gì hết luôn?
          Like that? You didn't know anything?

02 Lan: Lan khồng biết.
          I didn't know.

03 Diep: Không biết mặt luôn? Biết không?
          You didn't know his face? Didn't know?

04 Lan: Lan không có biết. Lan không có biết mặt.
          I didn't (have) know. I didn't know his face.

05 Diep: Vậy hả?
          Like that?

06 Lan: Tới hồi lúc mà ảnh nói với mẹ Lan,
          Till the time he spoke with my mother

07   Lan còn không biết mặt ảnh nữa mà.
          I still didn't know his face at all.

Clearly this is L's story, over which she has greater epistemic rights. More importantly, the events of the narrative are ones in which she exhibits a good deal of emotional involvement. Faced with a situation in which one important upshot of the story has been articulated by the story-recipient's question, the teller confirms with a repetition.

This qualitative evidence comparing Vietnamese and English – two widely separated, genetically unrelated languages – suggests that similar principles are at work in the linguistic formation of action in responding. Further support may be found in evidence from a large comparative project on question–answer sequences (Stivers et al. 2009), which measured relative frequency in conversational corpora of the interjection versus repetition forms of answering. According to our argument above, confirmation via repetition is semiotically marked, and so according to the usual properties of marked forms, it is likely to be less frequent. As predicted, the project found that in most languages, the interjection strategy is far more common than the repetition strategy (e.g., only 4 percent of answers in Danish are done by repetition, and only 13 percent in English; see Enfield et al. 2017 for details, and further discussion).

Agency in the Formation of Responsive Action

Our analysis of the functional differentiation in confirmation formats is supported by the evidence from context of use. In the case of certain rituals, such as the royal wedding with which we began, it can be observed that confirmation by repeat (rather than interjection) is more or less normatively required. Although the felicity conditions of the ritual might seem to require only the action of confirmation, with no restriction on what form that action takes, in practice repeat confirmations (e.g., *I will, I do*) are preferred and indeed constitute well-established and widely known formulae. When seen in the light of performative theories of ritual (e.g., Rappaport 1999, 2002; Tambiah 1985), this accords with our analysis. According to Rappaport and others, a ritual is effective to the extent that people participate in it and do so explicitly (preferably with witnesses and so on). That is, ritual effectiveness presupposes the active – or, agentive – engagement of the participants. In a highly consequential (status-changing) ritual such as a wedding, agentive participation is conveyed by repeat-formatted confirmation.

Our account suggests a general finding about agency – taken here to refer to a complex set of elements of an individual's flexibility and accountability in relation to action; cf. Kockelman (2007a, 2013), Enfield (2013) – in responsive action: to see one's degree of agency in response, look at how dependent the interpretation of the response turn's semantic/propositional content is on what has just been produced by the other speaker. For simplicity's sake, we will speak here of the elements of agency implied by Goffman's well-known distinction between the 'author', 'animator', and 'principal' components of speaker-hood (1979). Thus, if he says *Was it cool?*, when she says *Yeah*, then the content of what she's saying has actually been entirely authored and animated by him in the prior turn; she's just saying *Look back at what he just said and you'll see what I'm saying*. At the other extreme, if she says *It was cool* then she's explicitly asserting the entire semantic/proposi-tional content within the form of her own turn, and thus her turn is formulated as if she had said it independently, and thus, prior context (i.e., his prior turn) is not needed for the interpretation of what she is saying with her second-position move.

The alternatives for confirmation can be seen to vary in this way. For instance, in relation to the example just discussed, a response of *It was* would be less dependent for its semantic resolution on the prior turn than *Yeah*, but more dependent than saying *It was cool*. Adding 'cool' gives the second-position speaker some ownership via the fact that she has animated the key predicate; stressing a finite auxiliary gives second-position speaker ownership over the fact that she is *asserting* this proposition (see Stivers 2005); going further and replacing the prior turn's predicate, e.g., with *rad*, adds a re-authoring, thus implying independent access to the state of affairs being described, etc. Thus, while it is possible to understand this in scalar agency terms, one should not lose sight of the fact that agency is made up of multiple components. It is not just a scale from less to more (see Enfield 2013).

We have proposed a natural semiotic analysis of the functional differentiation and associated meanings of alternate formats for the confirmation of polar questions, as kinds of actions in interaction. Although we have drawn primarily on records of English conversation, because the analysis is based on principles of natural meaning – iconicity and indexicality – it should hold cross-linguistically. We predict that in all languages interjection confirmations will tend to accept the terms of the question to which they respond, whereas repeat confirmations will be more assertive.

Postface

The *sine qua non* of any theory is to explain a set of facts in relation to a smaller set of facts. All theories are reductive. Still we must be on guard against the tendency to over-generalize in thinking about language and action. Most linguistic theories – indeed most theories of language more generally, whether linguistic or philosophical in outlook – seek to identify a singular essence of language which can provide a key to understanding the whole. In generative grammar an entire theory of language was at one time (perhaps implicitly) built around the rules governing co-reference of anaphors and reflexives. In linguistic pragmatics, Searle presented his celebrated theory of speech acts through a consideration of promising. In linguistic anthropology, deictic terms and other indexicals were seen as expressing the essence of language.

In the history of linguistics, nowhere is this generalizing tendency seen more clearly than in the work of Ferdinand de Saussure. For Saussure, the key to understanding language – or *langue* – is the notion of value. Drawing particularly on the example of closed grammatical classes of pronouns, tense and aspect markers, as well as tightly organized lexical sets, Saussure argued that the meaning of any individual linguistic item, whether it be a word, a grammatical category, or syntactic construction, derives from its place in a system of oppositions.[1] With a series of startling examples, Saussure shows that the meaning of even the most seemingly name-like term does not derive from the real-world object to which it refers. Saussure tells us, for instance, that in some languages it is not possible to talk about 'sitting in the sun', for in these languages the word for 'sun' simply does not encompass the set of meanings that would allow for such a usage (unlike, in that respect, English *sun*, or French *soleil*). Language then is 'un système où tout se tient', as Meillet is supposed to have said (see Koerner 1996).

While Wittgenstein argues just as vigorously against the view that language is a nomenclature – i.e., just a list of names for things – his reasons are different and he comes to radically different conclusions. In the second section of his *Philosophical Investigations*, Wittgenstein offers a deceptively simple example in which he imagines a builder communicating with his assistant by calling out simple words like 'block' and 'slab':

The language is meant to serve for communication between a builder A and an assistant B. A is building with building stones: there are blocks, pillars, slabs and beams. B has to pass the stones, and that in the order in which A needs them. For this purpose they use a language consisting of the words 'block', 'pillar', 'slab', 'beam'. A calls them out; – B brings the stone which he has learnt to bring at such-and-such a call.

In Wittgenstein's example, people are using language to accomplish tasks that are constitutive of the activity of building. On this view language is necessarily linked to the activities in which it is used, and linked to those actions for which it serves as the vehicle, for instance, requests, orders, and instructions.

---

[1] One of Saussure's examples involves the words denoting mental states such as fear and dread. Comparison could be made here with Wittgenstein who discusses just such words in his famous argument against a 'private language'.

Wittgenstein introduced the notion of 'language game' to refer to language and 'the actions into which it is woven'. As is well known, the later Wittgenstein suggested that we examine language in relation to its contexts of use. He claimed in his last writings that 'our talk gets its meaning from the rest of our proceedings' (1969:#229). He illustrates the importance of such contexts of use by elaborating the 'slab-beam' game. He adds colour terms and words which function as numbers:

Besides the four words 'block', 'pillar', etc., let it contain a series of words used as [...] numerals (it can be the series of letters of the alphabet); further let there be two words, which may as well be 'there' and 'this' (because this roughly indicates their purpose), that are used in connexion with a pointing gesture; and finally a number of colour samples. A gives an order like: 'd-slab-there'. At the same time he shews the assistant a colour sample, and when he says 'there' he points to a place on the building site. From the stock of slabs B takes one for each letter of the alphabet up to 'd', of the same colour as the sample, and brings them to the place indicated by A. On other occasions A gives the order 'this-there'. At 'this' he points to a building stone. And so on.

Wittgenstein here draws our attention to the fact that the various components of a language and of particular language games are highly differentiated. Whereas Saussure gives us a picture of language in which a few examples are made to stand for the whole, Wittgenstein denies that there is an essence of language that might serve as the basis for such generalization. For Wittgenstein there is no particular linguistic sign nor any more abstract feature of language (such as value) that could stand for the whole. Rather, language exhibits a kind of radical heterogeneity.

This heterogeneity can be difficult to see if our native linguistic ideologies get in the way. Linguistic forms exhibit a superficial similarity which can easily lead us to imagine that linguistic signs are more homogeneous than they really are: In spoken language, signs are composed of phonic substance patterned in regular ways according to the phonological rules and constraints of a language. As Wittgenstein memorably describes, looking at a language 'is like looking into the cabin of a locomotive':

There are handles there, all looking more or less alike. (This stands to reason, since they are all supposed to be handled.) But one is the handle of a crank, which can be moved continuously (it regulates the opening of a valve); another is the handle of a switch, which has only two operative positions: it is either off or on; a third is the handle of a brakelever, the harder one pulls on it, the harder the braking; a fourth, the handle of a pump: it has an effect only so long as it is moved to and fro.

(Wittgenstein 1953, I, §2)

The words of a language are like the handles in Wittgenstein's cabin: We only see the parts which are to be grasped, and so all look like the same basic kind of device. But deeper examination reveals that each handle is linked to quite different causal mechanisms, in different parts of the engine (see Figure P.1):

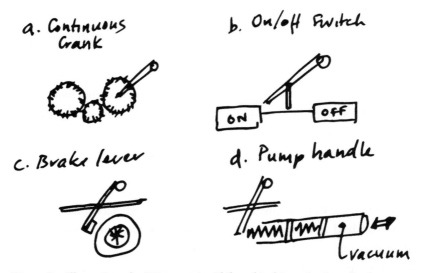

a. Continuous Crank

b. On/off Switch

ON OFF

c. Brake lever

d. Pump handle

vacuum

Figure P.1 Illustrations for Wittgenstein, *Philosophical Investigations*, Section 12.

Like handles in an engine room, words may exhibit a superficial similarity. But this is deceptive. To understand the elements of language, we cannot look at their appearance. We must look and see what they do and how they do it. And to see this is to see that Wittgenstein was right (see also Zipf 1949):

Think of the tools in a tool-box: there is a hammer, pliers, a saw, a screw-driver, a rule, a glue-pot, glue, nails and screws. The functions of words are as diverse as the functions of these objects. (And in both cases there are similarities.) Of course, what confuses us is the uniform appearance of words when we hear them spoken or meet them in script and print. For their application is not presented to us so clearly.

(Wittgenstein 1953, I, §8)

As both Saussure and Wittgenstein argued, and many others since (perhaps most notably Jakobson 1960 and Silverstein 1976), we must free ourselves from the pervasive misconception that language is fundamentally a system of names for objects in the world. That view is widely expressed, as a matter of course and without reflection. As Li and Gleitman (2002:266), for example, put it, language is a 'means for making reference to the objects, relations, properties, and events that populate our everyday world.' This kind of remark in the linguistic literature is as common as an old shoe. But the truth is that making reference is merely a fraction of what language does. Just about every move we make in navigating the social relationships that define us is made using the vehicle of talk. We coerce, cajole, and command. We ask, accept, and agree. We gossip and goad. Language provides our most important tools for carrying out social life.

*

In this book we have argued for the composite, situated, token nature of action, carried out through language. Our argument is intended to suggest a programme of research into the semiotics of natural languages as a key resource for the formation and interpretation of human action in interaction. It is a programme based on the primary use of language in naturally occurring, multi-modal, relationship-grounded, culturally situated social life.

If we are going to understand the nature, extent, and limits of linguistic and cultural diversity and their consequences for human action, this will require extensive research into the countervailing forces of natural meaning on the one hand, and historically shaped diversification on the other, as these are realized in and through interaction. It will require concerted efforts from linguistics, conversation analysis, and linguistic anthropology together. From linguistics we have detailed lexico-grammatical analysis and a framework for structural description. From conversation analysis we have a method for the rigorous description of interaction. And from linguistic anthropology we have a semiotic theory of language and culture. Together these traditions provide the tools we need to develop a realistic account of language as a resource for social action.

We conclude by returning to three central proposals upon which our concept of action is based. First: Human conduct is goal-directed and purposive. Second: This is a fundamental assumption that any person uses in interpreting what another person is up to (independent from what that person might actually be up to). And third: Much if not most action ascription is achieved in an enchronic frame by virtue of the way a response to some conduct *treats* that conduct, not necessarily how it *describes*, or might describe, that conduct. Actions can be appropriately responded to, based on interpretation of the often multiple semiotic features used, without them having been labelled or 'identified' at any level. People are often moved to use techniques that allow them to pursue a goal yet without being seen to have implemented an accountable action directly associated with that goal.

But action description is always possible. We need it, for example, for characterizing, scrutinizing, or reporting what people do. In this way, agents operate within a web of *potentially* describable actions, and thus under a tyranny of accountability. Such is the nature of action.

References

Ackrill, J. 1978. Aristotle on action. *Mind* 87(4):595–601.

Agha, A. 1994. Honorification. *Annual Review of Anthropology* 23:277–302.

    2007. *Language and Social Relations*. Cambridge: Cambridge University Press.

Ahearn, L. 2001. Language and agency. *Annual Review of Anthropology* 30:109–37.

Anscombe, G. E. M. 1957. *Intention*. Oxford: Basil Blackwell.

    1979. Under a description. *Noûs* 13(2):219–33.

Austin, J. L. 1962. *How to Do Things with Words*. Cambridge, MA: Harvard University Press.

Bloomfield, L. 1933. *Language*. New York: Holt.

Boas, F. 1911. Introduction. In F. Boas, ed., *The Handbook of American Indian Languages*, pp. 3–83. Washington, DC: Bureau of American Ethnology.

Boroditsky, L. 2001. Does language shape thought? English and Mandarin speakers' conceptions of time. *Cognitive Psychology* 43(1):1–22.

Bourdieu, P. 1977. *Outline of a Theory of Practice*. Cambridge: Cambridge University Press.

Briggs, C. 1986. *Learning How to Ask: A Sociolinguistic Appraisal of the Role of the Interview in Social Science Research*. Cambridge: Cambridge University Press.

Brown, R., and A. Gilman. 1960. The pronouns of power and solidarity. In T. Sebeok, ed., *Style in Language*, pp. 253–76. Cambridge, MA: MIT Press.

Clark, A. 2007. *Supersizing the Mind: Embodiment, Action, and Cognitive Extension*. New York: Oxford University Press.

Clark, H. H. 1996. *Using Language*. Cambridge: Cambridge University Press.

    2006. Social actions, social commitments. In N. J. Enfield and Stephen C. Levinson, eds., *Roots of Human Sociality: Culture, Cognition, and Interaction*, pp. 126–52. London: Berg.

Curl, T., and P. Drew. 2008. Contingency and action: A comparison of two forms of requesting. *Research on Language & Social Interaction* 41:129–53.

Davidson, D. 1963. Actions, reasons, and causes. *Journal of Philosophy* 60 (23):685–700.

　　1978. Intending. In Yirmiahu Yovel, ed., *Philosophy of History and Action*, pp. 41–60. Dordrecht: D. Reidel.

Dresher, E. 1995. There's no reality like psychological reality. *Glot International* 1(1): 7.

Drew, P. 1991. Asymmetries of knowledge in conversational interactions. In I. Markova and K. Foppa, eds., *Asymmetries in Dialogue*, pp. 29–48. Hemel Hampstead: Harvester Wheatsheaf.

　　1997. 'Open' class repair initiators in response to sequential sources of trouble in conversation. *Journal of Pragmatics* 28:69–101.

　　2004. Conversation analysis. In K. Fitch and R. Sanders, eds., *Handbook of Language and Social Interaction*, pp. 71–102. Mahwah, NJ: Lawrence Erlbaum.

Dunbar, R. I. M. 1996. *Grooming, Gossip and the Evolution of Language*. London: Faber and Faber.

Duranti, A. 1990. Politics and grammar: Agency in Samoan political discourse. *American Ethnologist* 17(4):36–56.

　　2004. Agency in language. In A. Duranti, ed., *A Companion to Linguistic Anthropology*, pp. 451–73. Malden: Blackwell.

　　2015. *The Anthropology of Intentions: Language in a World of Others*. Cambridge: Cambridge University Press.

Enfield, N. J. 2005. Areal linguistics and mainland Southeast Asia. *Annual Review of Anthropology* 34:181–206.

　　2006. Social consequences of common ground. In N. J. Enfield and S. C. Levinson, eds., *Roots of Human Sociality: Culture, Cognition and Interaction*, pp. 399–430. Oxford: Berg.

　　2007a. *A Grammar of Lao*. Berlin: Mouton de Gruyter.

　　2007b. Meanings of the unmarked: How 'default' person reference does more than just refer. In N. J. Enfield and T. Stivers, eds., *Person Reference in Interaction: Linguistic, Cultural and Social Perspectives*, pp. 97–120. Cambridge: Cambridge University Press.

　　2009. *The Anatomy of Meaning: Speech, Gesture, and Composite Utterances*. Cambridge: Cambridge University Press.

　　2011. Elements of action ascription: A generative account? Paper presented at the Workshop on Proposals and Action Ascription in Conversation, Max Planck Institute for Psycholinguistics, 17–20 March 2011.

　　2013. *Relationship Thinking: Agency, Enchrony, and Human Sociality*. Oxford: Oxford University Press.

　　2014a. *Natural Causes of Language: Frames, Biases, and Cultural Transmission*. Berlin: Language Science Press.

References

2014b. Human agency and the infrastructure for requests. In P. Drew and E. Couper-Kuhlen, eds., *Requesting in Social Interaction*, pp. 35–53. Amsterdam: John Benjamins.

2015. Linguistic relativity from reference to agency. *Annual Review of Anthropology* 44:207–44.

2017. Language in the mainland Southeast Asia area. In R. Hickey, ed., *The Cambridge Handbook of Areal Linguistics*, pp. 677–702. Cambridge: Cambridge University Press.

Enfield, N. J., and G. Diffloth. 2009. Phonology and sketch grammar of Kri, a vietic language of Laos. *Cahiers de Linguistique Asie Orientale* 38(1):3–69.

Enfield, N. J., and P. Kockelman (eds.). 2017. *Distributed Agency*. New York: Oxford University Press.

Enfield, N. J., and S. C. Levinson. 2006. Introduction: Human sociality as a new interdisciplinary field. In N. J. Enfield and S. C. Levinson, eds., *Roots of Human Sociality: Culture, Cognition, and Interaction*, pp. 1–38. Oxford: Berg.

Enfield, N. J., and J. Sidnell. 2012. Collateral effects, agency, and systems of language use. *Current Anthropology* 53:327–29.

2014. Language presupposes an enchronic infrastructure for social interaction. In D. Dor, C. Knight, and J. Lewis, eds., *The Social Origins of Language*, pp. 92–104. Oxford: Oxford University Press.

Enfield, N. J., T. Stivers, P. Brown, C. Englert, K. Harjunpää, M. Hayashi, T. Heinemann, G. Hoymann, T. Keisanen, M. Rauniomaa, C. W. Raymond, F. Rossano, K.-E. Yoon, I. Zwitserlood, and S. Levinson. 2017. Polar answers. Ms. submitted for publication.

Errington, J. 1985. On the nature of the sociolinguistic sign: Describing the Javanese speech levels. In E. Mertz and R. J. Parmentier, eds., *Semiotic Mediation: Sociocultural and Psychological Perspectives*, pp. 287–310. Orlando, FL: Academic Press.

1988. *Structure and Style in Javanese: A Semiotic View of Linguistic Etiquette*. Philadelphia: University of Pennsylvania Press.

Evans-Pritchard, E. E. 1937. *Witchcraft, Magic and Oracles among the Azande*. Oxford: Clarendon Press.

Everett C. 2013. *Linguistic Relativity: Evidence across Languages and Cognitive Domains*. Berlin/Boston: De Gruyter Mouton.

Finnegan, R. 1969. How to do things with words: Performative utterances among the Limba of Sierra Leone. *Man New Series* 4(4, Dec.): 537–52.

Fleming, L., and M. Lempert. 2014. Poetics and performativity. In N. J. Enfield, P. Kockelman, and J. Sidnell, eds., *Cambridge Handbook of Linguistic Anthropology*, pp. 485–515. Cambridge: Cambridge University Press.

Floyd, S., G. Rossi, J. Baranova, J. Blythe, M. Dingemanse, K. H. Kendrick, J. Zinken, and N. J. Enfield. 2014. Recruitments across languages: A systematic comparison. Paper presented at the Fourth International Conference on Conversation Analysis, University of California at Los Angeles.

Floyd, S., G. Rossi, and N. J. Enfield, eds. In press. *Getting People to Do Things: A Pragmatic Typology of Recruitments.* Berlin: Language Science Press.

Ford, C. E., B. A. Fox, and S. A. Thompson. 2002. Constituency and the grammar of turn increments. In N. J. Enfield and P. Kockelman, eds., *Distributed Agency*, pp. 14–38. New York: Oxford University Press.

Garfinkel, H. 1967. *Studies in Ethnomethodology.* Englewood Cliffs, NJ: Prentice-Hall.

Garfinkel, H., and H. Sacks. 1970. On formal structures of practical actions. In J. D. McKinney and E. A. Tiryakian, eds., *Theoretical Sociology*, pp. 337–66. New York: Appleton Century Crofts.

Geertz, C. 1973. *The Interpretation of Cultures.* New York: Basic Books.

Gell, A. 1998. *Art and Agency.* Oxford: Clarendon Press.

Gentner, D., and S. Goldin-Meadow. 2003. Whither whorf. In D. Gentner and S. Goldin-Meadow, eds., *Language in Mind: Advances in the Study of Language and Thought*, pp. 3–14. Cambridge, MA: MIT Press.

Giddens, A. 1993. *New Rules of Sociological Method*, 2nd edn. Stanford, CA: Stanford University Press.

Gigerenzer, G., R. Hertwig, and T. Pachur (eds.). 2011. *Heuristics: The Foundations of Adaptive Behavior.* New York: Oxford University Press.

Gipper, S. 2011. Evidentiality and intersubjectivity in Yurakaré: An interactional account. PhD dissertation, Radboud Universiteit, Nijmegen.

Gluckman, M. 1963. Gossip and scandal. *Current Anthropology* 4(3):307–16.

Goffman, E. 1957. Alienation from interaction. *Human Relations* 10:47–60.

1959. *The Presentation of Self in Everyday Life.* Garden City, NY: Doubleday.

1963. *Behavior in Public Places: Notes on the Social Organization of Gatherings.* New York: The Free Press.

1976. Replies and responses. *Language in Society* 5(3):257–313.

1979. Footing. *Semiotica* 25:1–29.

Goodwin, C. 1981. *Conversational Organization: Interaction between Speakers and Hearers.* New York: Academic Press.

1987. Unilateral departure. In G. Button and J. R. E. Lee, eds., *Talk and Social Organisation*, pp. 206–16. Clevedon: Multilingual Matters.

2000. Action and embodiment within situated human interaction. *Journal of Pragmatics* 32(10):1489–522.

2002. Time in action. *Current Anthropology* 43:(S)19–35.

References

2006. Human sociality as mutual orientation in a rich interactive environment: Multimodal utterances and pointing in aphasia. In N. J. Enfield and S. C. Levinson, eds., *Roots of Human Sociality: Culture, Cognition, and Interaction*, pp. 97–125. London: Berg.

Goodwin, C., and M. H. Goodwin. 1987. Concurrent operations on talk: Notes on the interactive organization of assessments. *IPrA Papers in Pragmatics* 1(1):1–52.

Goodwin, C., and J. Heritage. 1990. Conversation analysis. *Annual Review of Anthropology* 19:283–307.

Goodwin, M. H. 1990. *He-Said-She-Said: Talk as Social Organization among Black Children*. Bloomington: Indiana University Press.

Goody, Jack. 1977. *The Domestication of the Savage Mind*. Cambridge: Cambridge University Press.

Grice, H. P. 1989. *Studies in the Way of Words*. Cambridge, MA: Harvard University Press.

Gumperz, J. J., and S. C. Levinson (eds.). 1996. *Rethinking Linguistic Relativity*. Cambridge: Cambridge University Press.

Hacking, I. 1998. Making up people. In M. Biagioli, ed., *Science Studies Reader*, pp. 161–71. London: Routledge.

Haiman, J. 1985. *Natural Syntax*. Cambridge: Cambridge University Press.

Hakulinen, A., and M.-L. Sorjonen. 2009. Designing utterances for action: Ways of repeating the verb as a response to an assessment. In M. Haakana, M. Laakso, and J. Lindström, eds., *Talk-in-Interaction: Comparative Dimensions*, pp. 124–51. Helsinki: Finnish Literature Society.

Hanks, W. F. 1990. *Referential Practice: Language and Lived Space among the Maya*. Chicago, IL: University of Chicago Press.

Hayano, K. 2011. Claiming epistemic primacy: Yo-marked assessments in Japanese. In T. Stivers, L. Mondada, and J. Steensig, eds., *The Morality of Knowledge in Conversation*, pp. 58–81. Cambridge, Cambridge University Press.

2013. Territories of knowledge in Japanese conversation. Unpublished PhD thesis, Radboud University Nijmegen, Netherlands.

Hayashi, M., G. Raymond, and J. Sidnell. 2013. Introduction: Conversational repair and human understanding. In M. Hayashi, G. Raymond, and J. Sidnell, eds., *Conversational Repair and Human Understanding*, pp. 1–40. Cambridge: Cambridge University Press.

Heritage, J. 1984. *Garfinkel and Ethnomethodology*. Cambridge: Polity Press.

1998. Oh-prefaced responses to inquiry. *Language in Society* 27(3):291–334.

2002. Oh-prefaced responses to assessments: A method of modifying agreement/ disagreement. In C. E. Ford, B. A. Fox, and S. A. Thompson, eds., *The Language of Turn and Sequence*, pp. 196–224. Oxford: Oxford University Press.

2012. Epistemics in action: Action formation and territories of knowledge. *Research on Language and Social Interaction* 45:1–25.

2013. Action formation and its epistemic (and other) backgrounds. *Discourse Studies* 15:547–74.

Heritage, J., and G. Raymond. 2005. The terms of agreement: Indexing epistemic authority and subordination in talk-in-interaction. *Social Psychology Quarterly* 68(1):15–38.

2012. Navigating epistemic landscapes: Acquiescence, agency and resistance in responses to polar questions. In J. P. De Ruiter, ed., *Questions: Formal, Functional and Interactional Perspectives*, pp. 179–92. Cambridge: Cambridge University Press.

Hockett, C. F. 1960. The origin of speech. *Scientific American* 203:89–96.

Hutchins, E. 1995. *Cognition in the Wild*. Cambridge, MA: MIT Press.

2006. The distributed cognition perspective on human interaction. In N. J. Enfield and S. C. Levinson, eds., *Roots of Human Sociality: Culture, Cognition and Interaction*, pp. 375–98. Oxford: Berg.

Hutchins, E., and B. Hazlehurst. 1995. How to invent a shared lexicon: The emergence of shared form–meaning mappings in interaction. In E. Goody, ed., *Social Intelligence and Interaction: Expressions and Implications of the Social Bias in Human Intelligence*, pp. 53–67. Cambridge: Cambridge University Press.

Hymes, D. 1966. Two types of linguistic relativity (with examples from Amerindian ethnography). In W. Bright, ed., *Sociolinguistics, Proceedings of the UCLA Sociolinguistics Conference, 1964*, pp. 114–57. The Hague: Mouton.

Jacquemet, M. 1994. T-offenses and metapragmatic attacks: Strategies of interactional dominance. *Discourse and Society* 5(3):297–319.

Jakobson, R. 1960. Concluding statement: Linguistics and poetics. In T. A. Sebeok, ed., *Style in Language*, pp. 350–77. Cambridge, MA: MIT Press.

1990a. The speech event and the functions of language. In L. R. Waugh and M. Monville, eds., *On Language*, pp. 69–79. Cambridge, MA: Harvard University Press.

1990b. Shifters and verbal categories. In L. R. Waugh and M. Monville-Burston, eds., *On Language*, pp. 386–92. Cambridge, MA: Harvard University Press.

James, W. 1890. *Principles of Psychology*. New York: Henry Holt and Company.

Jefferson, Gail. 1980. On 'trouble-premonitory' response to inquiry. *Sociological Inquiry* 50:153–85.

2004. Glossary of transcript symbols with an Introduction. In G. H. Lerner (ed.), *Conversation Analysis: Studies from the First Generation*, pp. 13–23. Philadelphia, PA: John Benjamins.

References

2013. *Talking about Troubles in Conversation*. New York: Oxford Unviersity Press.

Jones, B. M. 1999. *The Welsh Answering System*. Berlin: Mouton de Gruyter.

Keevallik, L. 2010. Minimal answers to yes/no questions in the service of sequence organization. *Discourse Studies* 12(3):283–309.

Kendon, A. 1990. *Conducting Interaction: Patterns of Behavior in Focused Encounters*. Cambridge: Cambridge University Press.

2004. *Gesture: Visible Action as Utterance*. Cambridge: Cambridge University Press.

Kendrick, K. H., and P. Drew. 2016. Recruitment: Offers, requests, and the organization of assistance in interaction. *Research on Language and Social Interaction* 49(1):1–19.

Kidwell, M. 1997. Demonstrating recipiency: Knowledge displays as a resource for the unaddressed participant. *Issues in Applied Linguistics* 8:85–96.

2011. Epistemics and embodiment in the interactions of very young children. In T. Stivers, L. Mondada, and J. Steensig, eds., *The Morality of Knowledge in Conversation*, pp. 29–57. Cambridge: Cambridge University Press.

Kidwell, M., and D. H. Zimmerman. 2006. 'Observability' in the interactions of very young children. *Communication Monographs* 73(1):1–28.

Kockelman, P. 2005. The semiotic stance. *Semiotica* 157(1–4):233–304.

2006a. Representations of the world: Memories, perceptions, beliefs, intentions, and plans. *Semiotica* 162(1–4):73–125.

2006b. Residence in the world: Affordances, instruments, actions, roles, and identities. *Semiotica* 162(1–4):19–71.

2007a. Agency: The relation between meaning, power, and knowledge. *Current Anthropology* 48(3):375–401.

2007b. From status to contract revisited: Value, temporality, circulation and subjectivity. *Anthropological Theory* 7(2):151–76.

2013. *Agent, Person, Subject, Self: A Theory of Ontology, Interaction, and Infrastructure*. Oxford: Oxford University Press.

Koerner, E. F. K. 1996. Notes on the history of the concept of language as a system 'ou tout se tient'. *Linguistica Atlantica* 18/19:1–20.

König, E., and P. Siemund. 2007. Speech act distinctions in grammar. In T. Shopen, ed., *Language Typology and Syntactic Description*, 2nd edn. Cambridge: Cambridge University Press.

Langacker, R. W. 1987. *Foundations of Cognitive Grammar*. Vol. I: *Theoretical Prerequisites*. Stanford, CA: Stanford University Press.

Lave, J. 1988. *Cognition in Practice: Mind, Mathematics and Culture in Everyday Life*. Cambridge: Cambridge University Press.

Leach, E. R. 1968. Ritual. In D. Sills, ed., *International Encyclopedia of the Social Sciences*, Vol. XIII, pp. 520–6. New York. Macmillan and Free Press.

Leavitt, J. 2011. *Linguistic Relativities: Language Diversity and Modern Thought.* Cambridge: Cambridge University Press.

Lee, B. 1997. *Talking Heads: Language, Metalanguage, and the Semiotics of Subjectivity.* Durham, NC: Duke University Press.

Lee, S.-H. 2012. Response design in conversation. In J. Sidnell and T. Stivers, eds., *The Handbook of Conversation Analysis*, pp. 415–32. Boston, MA: Wiley-Blackwell.

2015. Two forms of affirmative responses to polar questions. *Discourse Processes* 52:21–46.

Levinson, S. C. 2005. Living with Manny's dangerous idea. *Discourse Studies* 7(4–5): 431–53.

2006. On the human 'interaction engine'. In N. J. Enfield and S. C. Levinson, eds., *Roots of Human Sociality: Culture, Cognition, and Interaction*, pp. 39–6. Oxford: Berg.

2012. Action formation and ascription. In J. Sidnell and T. Stivers, eds., *The Handbook of Conversation Analysis*, pp. 103–30. Malden, MA: Wiley-Blackwell.

2016. Speech acts. In Y. Huang, ed., *The Oxford Handbook of Pragmatics*, pp. 199–216. Oxford: Oxford University Press.

Levinson, S. C., and D. P. Wilkins (eds.). 2006. *Grammars of Space: Explorations in Cognitive Diversity.* Cambridge: Cambridge University Press.

Li, P., and L. Gleitman. 2002. Turning the tables: Language and spatial reasoning. *Cognition* 83(3):265–94.

Lucy, J. A. 1992a. *Language Diversity and Thought: A Reformulation of the Linguistic Relativity Hypothesis.* Cambridge: Cambridge University Press.

1992b. *Grammatical Categories and Cognition: A Case Study of the Linguistic Relativity Hypothesis.* Cambridge: Cambridge University Press.

1997. Linguistic relativity. *Annual Review of Anthropology* 26:291–312.

Majid, A., J. S. Boster, and M. Bowerman. 2008. The cross-linguistic categorization of everyday events: A study of cutting and breaking. *Cognition* 109(2):235–50.

Malinowski, B. 1935. *Coral Gardens and Their Magic.* Vol. II: *The Language of Magic and Gardening.* London: George Allen and Unwin.

McNeill, D. 2005. *Gesture and Thought.* Chicago, IL/London: University of Chicago Press.

Morgan, L. H. [1871] 1997. *Systems of Consanguinity and Affinity of the Human Family.* Lincoln: University of Nebraska Press.

Nietzsche, F. [1887] 1967. *On The Genealogy of Morals and Ecce Homo*, trans. and ed. Walter Kaufmann (translation of *On the Genealogy* in collaboration with R. J. Hollingdale). New York: Vintage.

References

Norman, D. A. 1988. *The Design of Everyday Things*. New York: Basic Books.

Ochs, E. 1988. *Culture and Language Development: Language Acquisition and Language Socialization in a Samoan Village*. Cambridge: Cambridge University Press.

1990. Indexicality and socialization. In J. Stigler, G. Herdt, and R. Shweder, eds., *Cultural Psychology: Essays on Comparative Human Development*, pp. 287–308. Cambridge: Cambridge University Press.

1992. Indexing gender. In A. Duranti and C. Goodwin, eds., *Rethinking Context: Language as an Interactive Phenomenon*, pp. 335–58. Cambridge: Cambridge University Press.

1996. Linguistic resources for socializing humanity. In J. Gumperz and S. C. Levinson, eds., *Rethinking Linguistic Relativity*, pp. 407–37. Cambridge: Cambridge University Press.

Parmentier, R. J. 1994a. Peirce divested for non-initiates. In *Signs in Society: Studies in Semiotic Anthropology*, pp. 3–22. Bloomington/Indianapolis: Indiana University Press.

1994b. Peirce's concept of Semiotic Mediation. In *Signs in Society: Studies in Semiotic Anthropology*, pp. 23–44. Bloomington/Indianapolis: Indiana University Press.

Pagel, M. 2012. *Wired for Culture: Origins Of The Human Social Mind*. New York: Norton.

Parsons, T. 1937. *The Structure of Social Action*. London: Collier-Macmillan.

Pederson, E., E. Danziger, D. G. Wilkins, S. C. Levinson, S. Kita, and G. Senft. 1998. Semantic typology and spatial conceptualization. *Language* 74(3):557–89.

Peirce, C. S. 1955. Logic as semiotic: The theory of signs. In J. Buchler, ed., *Philosophical Writings of Peirce*, pp. 98–120. New York: Dover.

Pomerantz, A. M. 1978. Compliment responses: Notes on the co-operation of multiple constraints. In J. Schenkein, ed., *Studies in the Organization of Conversational Interaction*, pp. 79–112. New York: Academic Press.

1980. Telling my side: 'Limited access' as a 'fishing device'. *Sociological Inquiry* 50: 186–98.

1984. Agreeing and disagreeing with assessments: Some features of preferred/ dispreferred turn shapes. In J. M. Atkinson and J. Heritage, eds., *Structures of Social Action: Studies in Conversation Analysis*, pp. 57–101. Cambridge: Cambridge University Press.

1986. Extreme case formulations: A way of legitimizing claims. *Human Studies* 9(2–3):219–29.

1988. Offering a candidate answer: An information seeking strategy. *Communication Monographs* 55(4):360–73.

Pomerantz, A., and J. Heritage. 2012. Preference. In J. Sidnell and T. Stivers, eds., *The Handbook of Conversation Analysis*, pp. 210–28. Boston: Wiley-Blackwell.

Quirk, R., S. Greenbaum, G. Leech, and J. Svartvik. 1985. *A Comprehensive Grammar of the English Language*. New York: Longman.

Rappaport, R. 1999. *Ritual and Religion in the Making of Humanity*. Cambridge: Cambridge University Press.

2002. Enactments of meaning. In M. Lambek, ed., *A Reader in the Anthropology of Religion*, pp. 446–67. Malden: Blackwell. (Excerpted from *Ritual and Religion in the Making of Humanity*, Cambridge University Press, 1999.)

Raymond, G. 2003. Grammar and social organization: Yes/no interrogatives and the structure of responding. *American Sociological Review* 68:939–67.

2013. At the intersection of turn and sequence organization: On the relevance of 'slots' in type-conforming responses to polar interrogatives. In B. Szczepek Reed and G. Raymond, eds., *Units of Talk: Units of Action*, pp. 169–206. Amsterdam: John Benjamins.

Raymond, G., and J. Heritage. 2006. The epistemics of social relations: Owning grandchildren. *Language in Society* 35:677–705.

Raymond, G., and J. Sidnell, 2014. Conversation analysis. In N. Coupland and A. Jaworski, eds., *The Discourse Reader*, 3rd edn, pp. 249–63. London/ New York: Routledge.

nd. Interaction at the boundaries of a world known in common: Initiating repair with 'what do you mean?' Ms.

Robinson, J. D. 2007. The role of numbers and statistics within conversation analysis. *Communication Methods and Measures* 1:65–75.

Rosaldo, M. Z. 1982. The things we do with words: Ilongot speech acts and speech act theory in philosophy. *Language in Society* 11(2):203–37.

Rosch, E. 1978. Principles of categorization. In E. Rosch and B. B. Lloyd, eds., *Cognition and Categorization*, pp. 27–48. Hillsdale, NJ: Lawrence Erlbaum.

Rossi, G. 2012. Bilateral and unilateral requests: The use of imperatives and Mi X? Interrogatives in Italian. *Discourse Processes* 49(5):426–58.

2014. When do people not use language to make requests? In P. Drew and E. Couper-Kuhlen, eds., *Requesting in Social Interaction*, pp. 303–34 (Studies in Language and Social Interaction, vol. 26). Amsterdam: John Benjamins.

2015. *The Request System in Italian Interaction* (MPI Series in Psycholinguistics, no. 99). Nijmegen: Radboud University Nijmegen.

Rossi, G., and J. Zinken. 2016. Grammar and social agency: The pragmatics of impersonal deontic statements. *Language* 92(4):e296–e325. doi:10.1353/lan.2016.0083.

Rumsey, A. 1990. Wording, meaning, and linguistic ideology. *American Anthropologist* 92(2):346–61.

References

Ryle, G. 1949. *The Concept of Mind*. London: Hutchinson.

Sacks, H. 1975. Everyone has to lie. In M. Sanches and Ben G. Blount, eds., *Sociocultural Dimensions of Language Use*, pp. 57–80. New York: Academic Press.

——— 1987. On the preferences for agreement and contiguity in sequences in conversation. In G. Button and J. R. E. Lee, eds., *Talk and Social Organisation*, pp. 54–69. Clevedon: Multilingual Matters.

——— 1995. *Lectures on Conversation*. Vols. I and II. Oxford: Basil Blackwell.

Sacks, H., E. A. Schegloff, and G. Jefferson. 1974. A simplest systematics for the organization of turn-taking for conversation. *Language* 50(4):696–735.

Sapir, E. 1921. *Language: An Introduction to the Study of Speech*. New York: Harcourt, Brace and Company.

——— 1933. La réalité psychologique des phonèmes. *Journal de Psychologie Normale et Pathalogique* (Paris) 30:247–65. English version published as 'The psychological reality of phonemes', in D. G. Mandelbaum, ed., *Selected Writings of Edward Sapir in Language, Culture and Personality*, pp. 46–60. Berkeley: University of California Press.

——— [1927] 1949. The unconscious patterning of behavior in society. In D. Mandelbaum, ed., *Selected Writings of Edward Sapir*, pp. 544–55. Berkeley: University of California Press.

——— [1931] 1964. Conceptual categories in primitive languages. In D. Hymes, ed., *Language in Culture and Society: A Reader in Linguistics and Anthropology*, p. 128. New York: Harper & Row.

Saussure, F. de. 1959. *Course in General Linguistics*. New York: McGraw-Hill.

Schegloff, E. A. 1968. Sequencing in conversational openings. *American Anthropologist* 70(6):1075–95.

——— 1986. The routine as achievement. *Human Studies* 9:111–51.

——— 1988. Goffman and the analysis of conversation. In P. Drew and A. J. Wootton, eds., *Erving Goffman: Exploring the Interaction Order*, pp. 89–135. Cambridge: Polity Press.

——— 1991. Conversation analysis and socially shared cognition. In L. Resnick, J. Levine, and S. Teasley, eds., *Perspectives on Socially Shared Cognition*, pp. 150–71. Washington, DC: American Psychological Association.

——— 1992. Repair after next turn: The last structurally provided defense of intersubjectivity in conversation. *American Journal of Sociology* 97(5):1295–345.

——— 1993. Reflections on quantification in the study of conversation. *Research on Language and Social Interaction* 26:99–128.

——— 1995. Discourse as an interactional achievement III: The omnirelevance of action. *Research on Language and Social Interaction* 28:185–211.

1996. Confirming allusions: Toward an empirical account of action. *American Journal of Sociology* 102(1):161–216.

1997. Practices and actions: Boundary cases of other-initiated repair. *Discourse Processes* 23(3):499–545.

2005. On complainability. *Social Problems* 52(3):449–76.

2006. Interaction: The infrastructure for social institutions, the natural ecological niche for language, and the arena in which culture is enacted. In N. J. Enfield and S. C. Levinson, eds., *Roots of Human Sociality: Culture, Cognition and Interaction*, pp. 70–96. Oxford: Berg.

2007. *Sequence Organization in Interaction: A Primer in Conversation Analysis*. Cambridge: Cambridge University Press.

2009. Prolegomena to the analysis of action(s) in talk-in-interaction. Paper presented at the LISO, University of California, Santa Barbara.

Schegloff, E. A., and G. H. Lerner. 2009. Beginning to respond: Well-prefaced responses to wh-questions. *Research on Language and Social Interaction* 42(2):91–115.

Schegloff, E. A., and H. Sacks. 1973. Opening up closings. *Semiotica* 8:289–327.

Schegloff, E. A., G. Jefferson, and H. Sacks. 1977. The preference for self-correction in the organization of repair in conversation. *Language* 53(2): 361–82.

Schelling, T. C. 1960. *The Strategy of Conflict*. Cambridge, MA: Harvard University Press.

Schutz, A. 1967. *Phenomenology of the Social World*. Evanston, IL: Northwestern University Press.

Searle, J. 1969. *Speech Acts*. Cambridge: Cambridge University Press.

1976. The classification of illocutionary acts. *Language in Society* 5(1):1–23.

1979. *Expression and Meaning*. Cambridge: Cambridge University Press.

1983. *Intentionality*. Cambridge: Cambridge University Press.

2006. Social ontology: Some basic principles. *Anthropological Theory* 6:12–29.

2010. *Making the Social World: The Structure of Human Civilization*. Oxford: Oxford University Press.

Sidnell, J. 2007a. Repairing person reference in a small Caribbean community. In N. J. Enfield and T. Stivers, eds., *Person Reference in Interaction: Linguistic, Cultural, and Social Perspectives*, pp. 281–308. Cambridge: Cambridge University Press.

2007b. Comparative studies in conversation analysis. *Annual Review of Anthropology* 36:229–44.

2009a. *Conversation Analysis: Comparative Perspectives*. Cambridge: Cambridge University Press.

References

2009b. Comparative perspectives in conversation analysis. In J. Sidnell, ed., *Conversation Analysis: Comparative Perspectives*, pp. 3–33. Cambridge: Cambridge University Press.

2009c. Language-specific resources in repair and assessments. In J. Sidnell, ed., *Conversation Analysis: Comparative Perspectives*, pp. 303–20. Cambridge: Cambridge University Press.

2010a. *Conversation Analysis: An Introduction*. Oxford: Wiley-Blackwell.

2010b. 'D'you understand that honey?': Gender and participation in conversation. In E. Stokoe and S. Speer, eds., *Conversation and Gender*, pp. 183–209. Cambridge: Cambridge University Press.

2012a. 'Who knows best?': Evidentiality and epistemic asymmetry in conversation. *Pragmatics and Society* 3(2):294–320. doi: 10.1075/ps.3.2.08sid.

2012b. Declaratives, questioning, defeasibility. *Research on Language and Social Interaction* 45(1):53–60.

2014. The architecture of intersubjectivity revisited. In N. J. Enfield, P. Kockelman, and J. Sidnell (eds.), *The Cambridge Handbook of Linguistic Anthropology*, pp. 364–99. Cambridge: Cambridge University Press.

Sidnell, J., and N. J. Enfield. 2012. Language diversity and social action: A third locus of linguistic relativity. *Current Anthropology* 53:302–33.

Sidnell, J., and M. Shohet. 2013. The problem of peers in Vietnamese interaction. *Journal of the Royal Anthropological Institute* 19(3):618–38.

Sidnell, J., and T. Stivers. 2012. Conversation analysis as an approach. In J. Sidnell and T. Stivers, eds., *The Handbook of Conversation Analysis*, pp. 1–7. Malden, MA: Wiley-Blackwell.

Silverstein, M. 1976. Shifters, linguistic categories, and cultural description. In K. Basso and H. Selby, eds., *Meaning in Anthropology*, pp. 11–55. Albuquerque: University of New Mexico Press.

1979. Language structure and linguistic ideology. In P. R. Clyne, W. F. Hanks, and C. L. Hofbauer, eds., *The Elements: A Parasession on Linguistic Units and Levels*, pp. 193–247. Chicago, IL: Chicago Linguistic Society.

1987. The three faces of 'function': Preliminaries to a psychology of language. In M. Hickmann, ed., *Social and Functional Approaches to Language and Thought*, pp. 17–38. Orlando, FL: Academic Press.

Sorjonen, M.-L. 1996. On repeats and responses in Finnish conversations. In E. Ochs, E. A. Schegloff, and S. A. Thompson, eds., *Interaction and Grammar*, pp. 277–327. Cambridge: Cambridge University Press.

2001. Simple answers to polar questions: The case of Finnish. In M. Selting and E. Couper-Kuhlen, eds., *Studies in Interactional Linguistics*, pp. 405–31. Amsterdam: John Benjamins.

References

Sorjonen, M.-L., and A. Hakulinen. 2009. Alternative responses to assessments. In J. Sidnell, ed., *Conversation Analysis: Comparative Perspectives*, pp. 281–303. Cambridge: Cambridge University Press.

Steensig, J., and T. Heinemann. 2013. When 'yes' is not enough – as an answer to a yes/no question. In B. Szczepek Reed and G. Raymond, eds., *Units of Talk: Units of Action*, pp. 207–42. Amsterdam: John Benjamins.

Stivers, T. 2005. Modified repeats: One method for asserting primary rights from second position. *Research on Language and Social Interaction* 38(2): 131–58.

   2011. Morality and question design: 'Of course' as contesting a presupposition of askability. In T. Stivers, L. Mondada, and J. Steensig, eds., *The Morality of Knowledge in Conversation*. pp. 82–106. Cambridge: Cambridge University Press.

Stivers, T., and N. J. Enfield. 2010. A coding scheme for question–response sequences in conversation. *Journal of Pragmatics* 42:2620–6.

Stivers, T., N. J. Enfield, P. Brown, C. Englert, M. Hayashi, T. Heinemann, et al. 2009. Universals and cultural variation in turn-taking in conversation. *Proceedings of the National Academy of Sciences* 106(26):10587–92.

Stivers, T., and M. Hayashi. 2010. Transformative answers: One way to resist a question's constraints. *Language in Society* 39(1):1–38.

Stivers, T., L. Mondada, and J. Steensig (eds.). 2011. *The Morality of Knowledge in Conversation*. Cambridge: Cambridge University Press.

Stivers, T., and J. D. Robinson. 2006. A preference for progressivity in interaction. *Language in Society* 35(3):367–92.

Stivers, T., and F. Rossano. 2010. Mobilizing response. *Research on Language and Social Interaction* 43(1):3–31.

Stivers, T., and J. Sidnell. 2016. Proposals for activity collaboration. *Research on Language and Social Interaction* 49(2):148–66.

Suchman, L. A. 1987. *Plans and Situated Actions: The Problem of Human-Machine Communication*. Cambridge: Cambridge University Press.

Tambiah, S. J. 1979. A performative approach to ritual. *Proceedings of the British Academy* 65:113–69; also in *Culture, Thought and Social Action: An Anthropological Perspective*, pp. 123–66. Cambridge, MA: Harvard University Press.

   1985. *Culture, Thought, and Social Action: An Anthropological Perspective*. Cambridge and London: MIT Press.

Tanney, J. 2009. *Rethinking Ryle: A Critical Discussion of the Concept of Mind*. Included in *The Concept of Mind* (60th Anniversary Edition). New York: Routledge.

References

Thompson, S. A., B. Fox, and E. Couper-Kuhlen. 2015. *Grammar in Everyday Talk: Building Responsive Actions*. Cambridge: Cambridge University Press.

Tomasello, M. 2008. *Origins of Human Communication*. Cambridge, MA: MIT Press.

 2009. *Why We Cooperate*. Cambridge, MA: MIT Press.

Tomasello, M., M. Carpenter, J. Call, T. Behne, and H. Moll. 2005. Understanding and sharing intentions: The origins of cultural cognition. *Behavioral and Brain Sciences* 28(5):664–70.

Velleman, J. David. 2015. *Foundations of Moral Relativism*. Open Book Publishers. www.openbookpublishers.com/reader/181#page/1/mode/2up.

Vilkuna, M. 1989. *Free Word Order: Its Syntax and Discourse Functions*. Helsinki: Finnish Literature Society.

Weber, M. [1947] 1961. Social action and its types. In T. Parsons, E. Shils, K. D. Naegele, and J. R. Pitts, eds., *Theories of Society*, Vol. I, pp. 173–9. New York: Free Press of Glencoe.

Whorf, B. L. [1939] 1956a. The relation of habitual thought and behavior to language. In John Carroll, ed., *Language, Thought, and Reality: Selected Writings of Benjamin Lee Whorf*, pp. 134–59. Cambridge, MA: MIT Press.

 [1940] 1956b. Science and linguistics. In J. Carroll, ed., *Language, Thought, and Reality: Selected Writings of Benjamin Lee Whorf*, pp.207–19. Cambridge, MA: MIT Press.

 [1945] 1956c. Grammatical categories. In J. Carroll, ed., *Language, Thought, and Reality: Selected Writings of Benjamin Lee Whorf*, pp.87–101. Cambridge, MA: MIT Press.

Wierzbicka, A. 1987. *English Speech Act Verbs: A Semantic Dictionary*. Sydney: Academic.

 2003. *Cross-Cultural Pragmatics: The Semantics of Human Interaction*. Expanded 2nd edn. Berlin: Mouton de Gruyter.

 2010. *Experience, Evidence, and Sense: The Hidden Cultural Legacy of English*. New York: Oxford University Press.

Winawer, J., N. Witthoft, M. Frank, L. Wu, A. Wade, and L. Boroditsky. 2007. Russian blues reveal effects of language on color discrimination. *Proceedings of the National Academy of Sciences of the USA* 104(19):7780–5.

Winford, D. 1993. *Predication in Caribbean English Creoles*. Amsterdam: John Benjamins.

Wittgenstein, L. 1953. *Philosophical Investigations*, ed. G. E. M. Anscombe and R. Rhees, trans. G. E. M. Anscombe. Oxford: Blackwell.

 1967. *Ludwig Wittgenstein: Zettel*, ed. G. E. M. Anscombe and G. H. von Wright, trans. G. E. M. Anscombe. Oxford: Blackwell.

References

1969. *On Certainty* [*Uber Gewissheit*], ed. G. E. M. Anscombe and G. H. von Wright, trans. D. P. and G. E. M. Anscombe. Oxford: Basil Blackwell.

[1956] 1978. *Remarks on the Foundations of Mathematics*, ed. G. H. von Wright, R. Rhees, and G. E. M. Anscombe, trans. G. E. M. Anscombe. Oxford: Blackwell.

1980. *Remarks on the Philosophy of Psychology*, Vol. II, ed. G. H. von Wright and H. Nyman, trans. C. G. Luckhardt and M. A. E. Aue. Oxford: Blackwell.

Zinken, J. 2016. *Requesting Responsibility*. New York: Oxford University Press.

Zinken, J., and E. Ogiermann. 2013. Responsibility and action: Invariants and diversity in object requests in Polish and British English interaction. *Research on Language and Social Interaction* 46(3):256–76.

Zinken, J., and G. Rossi. 2016. Assistance and other forms of cooperative engagement. *Research on Language and Social Interaction* 49(1):20–6.

Zipf, G. K. 1949. *Human Behavior and the Principle of Least Effort*. Cambridge, MA: Addison-Wesley.

Index

Index

Index